Thomas Gaskell Shearman

Natural Taxation

An Inquiry into the Practicability, Justice and Effects of a Scientific and....

Thomas Gaskell Shearman

Natural Taxation

An Inquiry into the Practicability, Justice and Effects of a Scientific and....

ISBN/EAN: 9783337060473

Printed in Europe, USA, Canada, Australia, Japan

Cover: Foto ©Suzi / pixelio.de

More available books at **www.hansebooks.com**

NATURAL TAXATION

AN INQUIRY INTO THE PRACTICABILITY, JUSTICE
AND EFFECTS OF A SCIENTIFIC AND
NATURAL METHOD OF
TAXATION

BY

THOMAS G. SHEARMAN

G. P. PUTNAM'S SONS
NEW YORK   LONDON
27 WEST TWENTY-THIRD STREET   24 BEDFORD STREET, STRAND

The Knickerbocker Press

1897

CONTENTS.

CHAPTER		PAGE
I.	Introductory	1
II.	Crooked Taxation	6
III.	Direct Taxation	39
IV.	Taxation of Personal Property	49
V.	Testimony of Experience	70
VI.	Effect of the Personalty Tax on Farmers	84
VII.	Taxation of Women and Children	101
VIII.	Taxation of Improvements	106
IX.	The Natural Tax	115
X.	One Tax Enough	136
XI.	Justice of Natural Taxation	165
XII.	Where the Burden Falls	174
XIII.	Social Effects of Natural Taxation	199
Index		225

NATURAL TAXATION.

CHAPTER I.

INTRODUCTORY.

§ 1. **Is there any natural taxation?** Is there any such thing as a natural or strictly scientific method of taxation? Almost all self-styled practical men scornfully deny that there is; and in this denial, for once, the professors of economic science, whom they contemn, seem to agree with them. It is more than doubtful whether any such writer upon the subject recognizes any natural form of taxation; while Professor Perry distinctly asserts: "There can be no science of taxation"; and: "Nature has given no whisper, that we can hear, about any taxes.[1]" Professor Sumner also says: "There are no natural laws of taxation." Of course, all good protectionists cordially indorse these opinions.

Nevertheless, is this consensus of opinion well founded? Is it true that Nature has nothing to say on this subject? Is it true that there is and can be no science of taxation? If it is, then Nature can have nothing to say about government, and all talk of the science of government is folly. For government implies taxation, as truly as the

---

[1] Perry's *Pol. Economy* (20th ed.), 581.

existence of animated nature implies food. Taxation is the indispensable condition of all government. Taxes are the food upon which it lives. Without taxes it must die. If all offices of government were filled gratuitously, it would none the less be maintained by taxation, although the only direct taxpayers would be the office-holders. Just as certainly as the existence of the body implies a science of food, the existence of human society implies a science of taxation.

For society and civilization, the value of which is beyond all computation, cannot exist without government, and government cannot exist without taxation. If there is any real social science, that science must include all things which are essential to the existence of society. If it is true that taxation is necessary, that it is, upon the whole, productive of good, even under its present chaotic conditions, and that it does return an equivalent to society, does it not follow that a thing so necessary and so naturally beneficial can be brought into harmony with natural laws and organized upon a basis of principle? To say that it never can be, simply because no one has yet defined the principle upon which it should rest, is almost as absurd as to say that the law of gravitation did not exist until Newton invented it. Gravitation in the universe is not more inevitable than taxation in civilized society. We may be sure that there is a science of taxation, and that Nature has much to say about it, if we will only listen to her voice.

How can we learn the teachings of Nature upon this subject? How does Nature teach us anything? Is it not by the stern pressure of necessity, driving us forward, while every path, except the right one, is hedged up with difficulties and penalties? Nature tells us nothing, in plain words, but while, on the one hand, she makes it impossible for us to stand still, she walls up, on the other hand, the door to every wrong path. It is an invisible wall, against which we blindly dash ourselves, again and again, until at last we learn the lesson and grope our way to the only open door. Even so, Nature shuts the door in our faces, as we try one method of taxation after another; until at last we stumble upon a path, the door of which is wide open, and which is not obstructed by insuperable obstacles. Then, it may be, we shall find not only that the method of taxation thus indicated is the easiest and best one, but also that Nature has all along collected taxes by this method, while we have wasted our efforts in double taxation, to the vast injury of the whole human race.

Let us then, before seeking to find a method affirmatively pointed out by Nature, inquire into the working and effects of the methods commonly in use, and the testimony of experience as to their results.

§ 2. **Bad effects of existing system.** The condition of society, in the most highly civilized countries, is sufficient proof that Christianity and civilization have thus far failed to produce the beneficial effects which might reasonably be expected of them. A few absurd optimists strive to convince us that all is for the best, in this best of all possible worlds; but the common-sense of mankind, and especially of the prosperous classes themselves, is fully convinced that there is something radically wrong in our civilization. Analogies must not be pushed too far; but they must be used, though not abused. When a sensible physician is called to advise upon a case of chronic indigestion, his first inquiry is concerning the food upon which the patient has lived. Bad food may not be the only cause; but if the patient's food is clearly bad, the physician reforms that, before he attempts to reform anything else. When we find society in an unhealthy state, wealth unequally and unjustly distributed, idle people rich, industrious people poor, gambling encouraged, industry and commerce discouraged, desperate and degrading poverty side by side with excessive and wasted wealth, it is not a mere delusion, as some would have us believe, which leads us to say that these are the results of bad government. But when we seek for the causes of bad government, why should we not do as we would in the case of the human body, and ask upon what food this government has lived? Bad taxation is as certain to produce bad government and bad social conditions, as is bad food to produce indigestion and decay in the human body. And as no medicine, in the long run, can supply the place of good food, so no other social reforms can ever bring social health, so long as unjust and unscientific forms of taxation are continued.

§ 3. **Bad taxation destructive of society.** Just as the human body can sustain life for a long time upon poor food, taken irregularly, at wrong times, and in wrong proportions, so government can be sustained for an indefinite period upon bad taxes, oppressive, unjust, badly collected, and in many respects injurious. But, as bad food breaks down the health and shortens the life of the body, so bad taxes destroy the health and sometimes even the life of the state. The Roman Empire owed its destruction as much to bad taxation as to slavery itself.

What are bad taxes? Surely, all taxes are bad, which bear most heavily upon those who are least able to pay and who derive the least benefit from government. Any tax is bad, which takes from the poverty of the poor to add to the wealth of the rich. Any tax is bad, which can be easily evaded by fraud or falsehood, and is therefore paid only by the honest and truthful. Any tax is bad, which can only be collected by oppressive and degrading methods. Any tax is bad, which unnecessarily hinders the increase of wealth and comfort among the people as a whole. Any tax is bad, which corrupts the morals of the people or which necessarily brings into existence a class which finds its profit in promoting wastefulness and extravagance in public affairs. Finally, any tax is bad, which makes the real taxpayer pay it twice over, while the government receives it but once.

CHAPTER II.

CROOKED TAXATION.

§ 1. Faults of existing system. The system of taxation most in use, in all civilized countries to-day, has all these faults.

The taxes under this system are always paid to the government by persons who are authorized and expected to recover the amount from some one else, with interest and a profit, upon which the law places no limit.

No one can ever tell the precise amount actually contributed by any one person, under this system, to the support of government.

No one can tell how much of the money paid by the final taxpayer goes to the support of the government, or how much goes into the private purses of individuals.

A large portion of the final tax-burden is invariably perverted to private use; while, in many cases, nine tenths and even nineteen twentieths are thus perverted.

Private property is thus forcibly taken for private use; an operation which every court in civilized countries declares in so many words to be "robbery, under the forms of law."[1]

The amount of the tax has only a remote connection with the actual needs or expenses of government. It may be and the fact has been, in several countries, for ten or twenty years together, either much more or much less

---

[1] U. S. Supreme Court, Loan Asso. v. Topeka, 20 Wallace, 655.

than the government needed. Where this is the sole method of taxation, taxpayers often pay a lighter tax, for years together, under an extravagant and even corrupt government, than they pay under one rigorously economical and honest. This is no accident; it is inherent in the system.

The pressure of such taxation, therefore, has almost no effect in educating the people to demand or appreciate good government.

The more wisely and honestly such a system is administered, the more popular does it make public extravagance and the more unpopular public economy.

§ 2. **Profits of crooked taxation.** Under such a system, a few persons make large profits; and they easily concentrate their power to perpetuate and extend it, in such ways as more and more to diminish the proportion of revenue which goes to the public use and to increase the proportion in which it is diverted to private use.

Under such a system, the persons who thus profit by what all courts of justice describe as " robbery, under the forms of law," acquire " vested interests "; interference with which is regarded, by multitudes of honest and unselfish men, as something positively wicked.

Thus, as a necessary result of this system, the right to live by robbery grows to be not merely equal but even superior to the right to live by labor. For the right of labor is not recognized by law or public opinion; while the right of robbery is.

Under this system, honest men are often forced to abandon honest labor, and to live upon legalized robbery. At first, this application of force is merely accidental; but eventually it is intentional and deliberate. It has been intentionally thus applied for a century, in America, and for at least two centuries in Europe.

§ 3. Taxation of poverty.

The whole burden of such taxes rests upon consumption and not at all upon wealth. The system absolutely exempts property from the support of government, and draws taxes only from those who have to spend, in proportion to their expenses.

Inasmuch as the necessary expenses of the very poor are a hundred times as large, in proportion to their wealth, as the necessary expenses of the very rich, these taxes bear with a hundred-fold severity upon the very poor, as compared with the very rich.

Averaging all classes of society under this system, the poor, as a class, invariably pay more than ten times their proper share of taxes; while the rich pay much less than one tenth of their proper share.

In addition to this, the system generally, though not invariably, adds to the cost of supporting the government a private profit, so large as to far exceed the whole amount of taxes paid by the rich as a class.

The whole of this private profit goes to a portion of the richer class; thus exempting them, as a class, from all taxation, and giving them a larger net profit from the very fact of taxation.

This system, therefore, perpetually adds to the natural savings of the rich; while it almost swallows up the natural savings of the poor.

The tendency of this method of taxation is, therefore:

1. To make the rich richer, and the poor poorer;
2. To shift the burden of taxation from those best able to bear it to those least able;
3. To remove all checks upon the extravagance of government, by making the only persons who know that they pay taxes indifferent as to the amount of taxes, if not actually interested in maintaining needless taxes, for the sake of a profit upon their collection·

4. To force into existence a class of wealthy men, whose income depends upon legalized robbery;

5. To complicate the business of the country with taxation, so that enormous burdens are kept upon the people, for fear that "vested interests" will suffer if these burdens are lightened;

6. To promote bribery and corruption, by making business profits directly dependent upon political action.

§ 4. **Crookedness of the system.** A system of taxation which invariably produces such results is fitly described by the name of Crooked Taxation.

It is crooked in its operation, crooked in its form, crooked in its motives, crooked in its aims, crooked in its effects, and, as fits a system inherently crooked, it is especially crooked in its influence upon the well-being of society.

It is not merely indirect. A curve is indirect. A right angle is indirect. Yet each is regular in its form and leads to results which can be clearly foreseen and which are frankly acknowledged. But so-called indirect taxation is never uniform in rates or operation. It never proceeds upon any fixed line, whether straight or curved. It never arrives at the point which is its professed aim, and it is never meant to arrive there by those who control it. It never produces the chief results which are expected from it, even by its inventors, and never produces any of the results which they publicly profess to expect from it, except in rare cases, in which their secret calculations are entirely at fault. Its line of working is pulled up and down by selfish interests, at a thousand points, until it becomes so hopelessly crooked that nothing short of omniscience can foresee its results. It gives rise to endless frauds, and every effort to repress these frauds involves some new oppression upon the honest and the poor. Invented originally to enable governors to defraud the people, it has no political support, except the desire of the governing class to deceive the taxpayer as to the cost of government, the desire of the governed to evade their just share of taxation, and the determination of a small section of the people to use it as a means of plundering all the rest. Undoubtedly, a few *doctrinaires* sincerely advocate this system, from honest motives; but their support counts for absolutely nothing, except as a convenient excuse in the mouths of those who have selfish reasons for quoting them.

It is doubtless time to verify these broad assertions, for the benefit of those who have not studied the question. No one who has studied it, with care and ordinary intelligence, since the days of the man who cynically declared that the supreme art of taxation was to pluck the greatest amount of feathers with the least amount of squalling, can have failed to see most of these things for himself. The only justification which any honest, intelligent man has ever offered for crooked taxation is either: (1) that government must be maintained, and the people will not submit to straightforward taxation for its maintenance; or (2) that *every* form of taxation is equally oppressive and demoralizing in its effects.

Crooked taxation assumes a great variety of forms; but it is most familiar under the names of tariffs and excise taxes. It will simplify the discussion to confine illustration to these forms, although they are not the only ones. At the outset, let us take the duty on sugar, as it was maintained until 1890, and the tax on whisky, which is still supported by a majority of both our political parties. The one is a necessity, the other (except for manufacturing use) a luxury; and thus the two illustrate those two sides of the question.

§ 5. **Taxes upon sugar and whisky.** The tax upon foreign sugar is admittedly paid by our own people. For many years it averaged 70 per cent. of the cost, and amounted to nearly $60,000,000 per annum. In addition to this, about 180,000 tons were annually produced at home, the price of which to the consumer was increased by at least two cents a pound by the tariff, or about $8,000,000 in all. Either the whole of this $8,000,000 went into the pockets of a few sugar-planters, or, which is more probable, they only gained half of it, while the other half was wasted in misapplied human effort. The effect of crooked taxation, in this instance, was probably to provide $60,000,000 annually for public use, and, by incidental "robbery under the forms of law," to seize $4,000,000 of private property for private use and $4,000,000 more for no use at all, absolutely destroying it by putting it into labor as grossly misapplied as would be carrying bricks to sea and dropping them in the ocean.

The correctness of these figures and inferences will no doubt be vehemently disputed. But none of the disputants will be able to furnish figures any more correct; and thus the truth of the next proposition will be proved, to wit, that no one can tell how much of these taxes goes to the state, how much to private pockets, and how much to pure waste.

But this is a mere beginning. By one of those innumerable breaks in the wriggling line of crooked taxation, which are made on purpose to deceive and defraud the people, the sugar tax was suddenly raised to a prohibitory point on all sugar fit to eat. Thus our refiners were given an absolute monopoly; and the whole tax on eatable sugar, as distinguished from the crude article, was levied for the sole benefit of the Sugar Trust,—another instance of unqualified robbery under the forms of law, without a shred of pretence of government revenue.

These exactions, amounting to over $75,000,000 per annum, did not end here. The jobbers and retailers must collect an increase from their customers, to pay for interest on their advances and usual profits; all of which must be paid by the consumers of sugar.

Who are these consumers? And how is this vast burden apportioned among the people? Every family consumes sugar. In what proportion? According to their wealth or their income? These considerations have only a slight influence. A family worth only $5,000 will generally consume as much sugar as one worth $100,000; and frequently such a family will consume more than a family worth $10,000,000. We all know instances in which this is true. To say that the poor pay ten times as much of the sugar tax as the rich, in proportion to their respective accumulations, is an absurdly low estimate of the truth. The very poor pay ten thousand times as much, in proportion, as the very rich.

The last consideration applies equally to the tax on domestic whisky. The tax is collected, with a large profit, from consumers; and whisky is consumed in far greater quantities by the poor than by the rich; so that on this, also, the poor are taxed out of all proportion to the rich; while dealers, who are rich, as compared with the vast majority of our people, make a large profit upon the taxes, which they first pay but immediately collect from their customers.[1]

---

[1] It is often said that a tax on whisky is purely voluntary, and that it should not be regarded as a burden upon the poor, since they can escape it by practising abstinence. But this is a palpable fallacy. So long as indirect taxation is maintained, the masses *must* pay the bulk of it; because the rich never are numerous enough to pay, in taxes upon their consumption, one fourth of the needful revenue. In actual fact, they do not pay one tenth of it. If then the American masses should renounce liquors and tobacco, as they do largely in Italy, and absolutely in India, they would be taxed just as heavily upon their bread and salt, as the Italians and Indians are

Will any one pretend that those who ultimately pay these enormous taxes upon sugar and whisky have any idea of the amount which they contribute to the support of the government? Does the payment of such taxes have the smallest tendency to excite in the real taxpayers an interest in honest and economical government? Are not such taxes devised for the precise and avowed purpose of preventing the mass of voters from feeling the burden and becoming restive under it? Was there ever any motive for originally levying these taxes, other than the desire to blind the people to the cost of government, and to obtain money from them without their real consent? Is there any other good reason for maintaining a tariff for revenue only or an internal excise tax?

§ 6. Impossibility of economical government under crooked taxation.—Can such taxes be so levied, under the most honest administration, as to be " limited to the needs of government, economically administered?" The needs of government, thus defined, will often rise $40,000,000 in one year and fall $30,000,000 in the next. Suppose the entire revenue to be derived from sugar and whisky, which will serve just as well as to refer to a thousand similar taxes now existing. Suppose the government to require an increase of $40,000,000 in its revenue. Shall the taxes on these articles be instantly increased by $20,000,000 each? Such things have been done; but with what result? Speculators learn that the increase is to be made; they use corrupt means to secure such an increase as will insure profits to them; and they make gigantic fortunes at the expense of the poor, who cannot buy more than their daily needs. With irony, all the more bitter because it was so unconscious, our simple-minded " second Franklin " used to ask why farmers, clerks, and day-laborers, who objected to a tax on pig-iron, did not forthwith build hundred-thousand-dollar furnaces, so as to participate in the profits of iron-making. And perhaps some other philosopher may ask why sewing-women do not buy sugar by the ton, at low prices, to feed their children.

Not only would speculators profit by such advances in taxation, but no human wisdom would suffice to measure even approximately the advance which ought to be made in order to produce the needed revenue. No estimate would come within $5,000,000 of the actual result. Consumption might be reduced so much, by the increased cost, as to make a higher tax produce a smaller revenue. This has happened in cases without number. Or, in the effort to allow for this, the revenue might be increased to an excessive amount.

§ 7. **Difficulty of reducing crooked taxes.** Take the case of a needed reduction of revenue. Did we not struggle with this problem for twenty years? Do we need any illustrations of the almost insuperable difficulties of reducing crooked taxes? Vested interests have sprung up. Large investments have been made, upon the expectation that the inequalities of crooked taxation would be maintained indefinitely. Reduction of taxes means ruin to a few wealthy men. In 1807, all New England raged against the embargo and non-intercourse acts. But, when they were forced on New England by the South, New England merchants turned into manufacturers, and made the South pay heavy tribute. When the absurd embargo was repealed, the South supposed that it would do a favor to New England by repealing the non-intercourse acts also; but, to the astonishment of short-sighted politicians, this repeal was defeated by New England votes, controlled by the new manufacturing class. The South forced New England into an abnormal development of manufactures; and it has paid heavily for its folly, for eighty years since.

It is impossible thus to trifle with vast business interests. After crooked taxation has forced capital to seek its profits out of legalized plunder, those who have been driven by legislation to seek profit in this way will fight to the death to maintain the taxes through which they live. They are not to be blamed, any more than a Turkish pasha is to be blamed for extortion, when his master gives him only the choice between living by extortion or dying by the bowstring.

Again, it is impossible to tell beforehand what will be the effect of a reduction of crooked taxation. A very heavy reduction of the tariff in 1846 produced a large increase of revenue. But a much smaller reduction in 1857 produced a permanent deficit in revenue. Judicial corrections of treasury rulings, reducing duties upon steel blooms at one time, and upon steel wire at another time, *increased* the revenue upon each of these articles, from a few hundred dollars to about two millions. Crooked taxes are like crooked rifles; the only thing of which you can be sure is that they will *not* produce the effect which you expect of them.

The result is that crooked taxes forever produce either a great deal too much or a great deal too little. And as no government can go on under a perpetual deficiency, every government, which depends entirely upon crooked taxation, keeps up excessive taxes and surplus revenues, with the inevitable consequences—extravagance, waste, and corruption. The total abolition of protective duties would make no difference upon this point. Public waste and corruption are the necessary results of exclusive dependence upon crooked taxation.

§ 8. Political corruption. Crooked taxation offers such inducements to bribery and other forms of political corruption as to make them almost inevitable. Whatever may be the fact in other countries, experience proves that, in America, at all events, such corruption is an invariable attendant of such taxation.

In the United States, this fact is not merely admitted by all political parties: it is positively charged by each of them in all their leading organs of opinion, by all of their orators in election campaigns, and by most of their leading statesmen. The Republican National Convention of 1888 distinctly charged that the proposed Democratic revision of the tariff was dictated by the Whisky Trust. Every Republican State convention, every Republican newspaper and every Republican orator declared that the Democratic tariff of 1894 was dictated by the Sugar Trust and carried through Congress by actual bribery. It is an article of faith, with almost every American protectionist, that all efforts for reduction in protective duties are paid for with British gold. On the other hand, every Democratic convention, newspaper and orator asserted continuously, from 1888 onwards, that the Republican victories of 1880 and 1888 were secured by open and flagrant bribery of voters upon an enormous scale, and that the protectionist tariffs of 1883 and 1890 were carried through Congress by the expenditure, in each case, of over two million dollars, mostly in purchasing the election of Congressmen, but partly in influencing Congress itself. The third party has always believed that both parties were thus corrupted.

§ 9. Evidence of corruption. Some of the most important of these accusations are unquestionably true; for they have been admitted by the very parties accused. In December, 1880, the Vice-President-elect, at a public dinner given in honor of one of the most notorious corruptionists in the country, declared, amid laughter and cheers, that the guest of the evening had carried the decisive State of Indiana by the liberal use of "soap"—a slang phrase well understood by all to mean bribes to voters. In 1888 the same State was again carried by such open and admitted bribery, under written instructions from a person who formerly held a high public office, that the very President, who owed the vote of his State to the management of this official, refused to have anything further to do with him. On the other hand, the charge of bribery with respect to the final form of the tariff of 1894, passed by a Democratic Congress, was made as vigorously by Democrats as by Republicans; and the only plea of justification ever made by the small section of the party accused was that the bribe had been paid before the election of Congress, in order to help its election, and that nothing had been paid to individual Congressmen since the election.

Whatever moral difference there may be between the bribery of Congressmen and the bribery of their electors, it is clear that the injury to the community, in the result upon its business interests, is equally serious in either case, while the general effect of buying electors is worse than that of buying Congressmen. It is probable that the votes of Congressmen upon the final passage of a tariff bill are rarely purchased, but it is still more probable that many votes upon details of a bill are purchased. Of course, legal evidence of such facts is almost impossible to be had, but evidence entirely satisfactory to reasonable minds has been obtained as to Congressional votes, both for and against tariff changes.

Nor is such corruption by any means confined to tariff legislation. There is far more evidence of Congressional corruption in connection with the whisky tax than in connection with any tariff. The frequent and sudden increases of the tax on whisky between 1862 and 1866 were notoriously accompanied by large speculations in whisky, carried for the account of Congressmen by the whisky ring, and amounting to direct and gross bribery. The last increase of twenty cents in this tax, made in 1894, has been followed by an official exposure of the Whisky Trust accounts, showing an expenditure of $600,000 for "statistics" and $500,000 for "extraordinary legal expenses," most of which, it is admitted, was made in corrupting Congress into the old trick of increasing the tax, while exempting whisky on hand. The fact that this enormous expenditure was not rewarded by full success suggests the amount which must have been spent on former occasions, when such success was obtained.

§ 10. **Iniquitous methods of collection.** The methods by which nearly all crooked taxes are collected are always and everywhere iniquitous and disgraceful. Perhaps we ought to say that the methods by which the amount to be collected is ascertained are iniquitous, rather than the mere final act of collection. Any gentleman can, without a stain upon his character, use such force as the law may direct, to seize property, forfeited for non-payment of taxes. But no true gentleman can go through all the details of the work required by law and necessity, to ascertain the amount which ought to be collected under most forms of crooked taxation. And although a very large number of true gentlemen do administer the existing tax laws, without doing anything unworthy of their reputation, their administration is attended with greater injustice to the poor and the honest taxpayers than is that part of the administration which is entrusted to unscrupulous and brutal officials.

§ 11. **Collection of excise taxes.** Take what are usually called internal-revenue taxes, but which are more correctly termed excise taxes, as an illustration. It is impossible to administer the laws imposing these taxes, without the constant aid of spies, sudden searches of private premises, seizures of property, upon the slightest pretext, continual arrests upon suspicion, and enormous penalties for slight offences and even for honest mistakes. The punishment visited upon a land-owner, who suffers his land to be used for making one gallon of illicit whisky is literally a thousand times more severe than can be imposed upon him for suffering the land to be used as a haunt of highway robbers. The punishment prescribed by law and inflicted in fact for making the gallon of whisky is far more severe than the punishment ever imposed for atrocious acts of violence, not reaching the dignity of actual attempts to kill. In England, thousands of brutes have dashed their wives or mothers against walls or tables, breaking several ribs; not one of whom was ever punished with one fourth of the severity shown to the maker of illicit candles.

It is not surprising that, for more than a century after excise taxes became general in England, so that not only liquors, but also leather, glass, candles, bricks, and innumerable other articles could only be manufactured under the rigid espionage of public officers, the very name of "exciseman" became an object of universal hatred and contempt. It is not surprising that, in the mountain regions of the South, where a little whisky would naturally be made on every farm, the exciseman is generally hated, although too powerful and courageous to be despised.

§ 12. **Collection of tariff duties.** Tariffs on imported goods are administered on similar principles. Every person arriving at our ports must submit to an examination of his baggage, such as he would think degrading and intolerable if made by a city assessor. Ladies' dresses and underclothing are dragged out and spread upon the wharf for the inspection of a coarse crowd of dock laborers. A "faithful officer" searches them carefully, to see if they are sufficiently dirty to warrant the belief that they are in "actual use." The late Mrs. William Waldorf Astor (honor to her memory!) was the first woman who rebelled against this abominable practice and refused to pay a tax upon cleanliness. She successfully appealed to the Supreme Court against this disgusting standard of taxable character; but the outrage is still repeated, ten thousand times a year, by vigilant officers, who peer and pry into women's clothing and insist that it must be new, because it is not filthy.

On the slightest suspicion that a passenger has concealed dutiable goods, the law gives absolute power to the customs officers to strip the suspected person naked; and this power is habitually exercised. There is enough sense of decency in our officials to assign women to the duty of stripping women; but imagine the shame and torture which even such a search must inflict upon a sensitive and innocent woman. Of course, the customs officers would, with one voice, declare that no innocent woman was ever subjected to such an outrage; but such a statement is an insult to our common-sense. The mere fact that no woman has brought suit for damages on this account proves nothing. Few sensitive women would endure the added shame of relating their story in court; and as none of them could prove malice on the part of the searcher, no sensible lawyer would advise them to sue. The malice is in the law, not in the officers.

The oppressions which have been practised upon millions of poor immigrants arriving in the United States have never been even faintly described. For many years it was the uniform practice to make them pay enormous taxes upon every article, however trifling, which they had not actually used and soiled. Cases are well known in which a poor woman, who had only one pair of stockings (which she kept clean for landing, going barefoot on the ship,) was taxed 80 per cent. on this pair; and men, having only two suits of clothing, have been taxed upon one suit for more than it cost. Nine officers reported their names for honorable mention, on their joint seizure of two yards of flannel, which a poor Irish woman had kept clean until her arrival. These are but small instances of vast numbers of similar petty and contemptible extortions, which are carried on, not from corrupt motives, but in zeal for the enforcement of crooked taxation. Is it possible that men of refinement and honor can administer such regulations without degradation?[1]

[1] While these pages were passing through the press the following item appeared in the New York *Evening Post*, of April 18, 1895.

"Washington, April 18.—Accompanying the Treasury decision permitting ships to come up to New York harbor in the night and discharge passengers' baggage without taking out a special permit or hiring inspectors, a code of instructions for inspectors will be promulgated. This will set forth in plain terms that the intent of the law is to break up smuggling in the importation of merchandise, not to annoy and harass the honest travelling public.

"Several cases have come to the notice of the department recently showing that inspectors often mistake their duty in this particular. Within one month, three women who had been travelling abroad and brought home millinery for their own use were pounced upon as professional dressmakers trying to smuggle in goods for sale to their customers. Two of the accused were able to prove their innocence without much difficulty; but in the case of the third certain measurements were taken which convinced the inspectors that the gowns found in her trunks could not be hers, as they would not fit her figure. At her own suggestion, therefore, she dressed herself in the several garments, and submitted the results to expert judges named by the collector, who promptly decided that the inspectors were in error and sent her home in triumph.

"It is the desire of the present administration of the Treasury to break up this sort of thing."

§ 13. **Ad valorem taxes.** The only fair method of taxing any article is obviously by proportioning the tax to its value. Taxes, levied in strict proportion to weight or measure only, are so frightfully unjust to the poorer classes that no one attempts to justify them, except on the ground of necessity, to avoid the frauds which are common under the *ad valorem* plan. So impracticable is it to make all duties specific, that under the McKinley tariff itself, which was framed in 1890 by fanatical devotees of the specific system, more than half of the duties were *ad valorem*.

But, in order to avoid fraud and evasion under *ad valorem* taxes, the government is compelled to employ a small army of spies, to resort to all kinds of low tricks to ascertain prices, to treat all merchants as thieves and rogues, to require detailed statements about matters concerning which the declarants cannot possibly know anything, to impose enormous fines and penalties for errors which may be fraudulent or may be perfectly innocent, to put valuations upon goods which the officials know and admit to be utterly false and excessive, and in general to adopt methods of dealing with honest taxpayers which no business man could use without being expelled from all decent society. Blackmail, fraud, swindling, and enforced lying are regular methods of collecting the tariff revenue of the United States, not through the fault of the administrative officers, but as the necessary result of deliberate provisions of statute law. These words do but express, in plain English, what both Republican and Democratic Secretaries of the Treasury have stated in the decent obscurity of many-syllabled words.

§ 14. **Crooked taxation widens the social chasm.** The greatest evil resulting from such taxes remains to be considered. This is their effect upon the distribution of wealth, by making the rich richer and the poor poorer than they would be under direct taxation.

It will not be here asserted that the poor are growing absolutely poorer. Whether true or false, that statement is not here in issue. The point made is that crooked taxation makes the poor poorer than they would be under direct taxation, and that it continually widens the disparity between the rich and the poor.

Some of the inevitable incidents of such a system tend strongly in this direction. The intermingling of politics with business and the constant interference with production and consumption, which crooked taxes involve, would alone give continual opportunities for speculation, of which none but capitalists can ever avail themselves, and from which, therefore, none but capitalists can profit; while such profits are made chiefly at the cost of the poor. The uncertainty of operation, which always attaches to these taxes, making that which was crooked in its construction doubly crooked in its working, opening still larger opportunities to speculators, swells yet more the profits of capitalists at the expense of others. Changes in the text of the laws providing for such taxes are very frequent; and changes of interpretation are ten times as frequent. Every one of these offers to a few shrewd capitalists a fine harvest, out of the crops of the poor. When such opportunities for profit become gradually infrequent, the class accustomed to count upon them clamor for a revision of the law; and, no matter whether the revision is upward or downward, the engrossing clerks always make some innocent mistake, which is worth a million dollars at least to some lawyer, who, by a marvellous instinct, discovers the mistake almost before the ink is dry; while fifty new elements of crookedness are introduced by sly legislators, which escape public attention, until another set of capitalists have cleared as many million dollars out of the "accidental inequalities" of taxation.

These characteristics of such legislation are usually brought up in controversies over the issue between tariffs for revenue and tariffs for protection; but in reality they have little to do with that issue. They are inherent in all tariffs and in all taxes upon production and exchange. The principal reason why they have become associated with that particular controversy is that, under a protective tariff, there is always a large number of wealthy and influential people who can be induced to join in a demand for revision; while, under a tariff for revenue only, such a demand comes only from the few who profit by mere change, unless there is a substantial reason for it. Moreover, a tariff for revenue only is, for reasons not necessary now to state, a practical impossibility in any country which depends for its revenue upon indirect taxation alone; and therefore the United States have never had any experience of it.

But all these effects of crooked taxation, amounting, though they do, to many millions, annually drawn from the poor and divided among a few of the rich, are insignificant; compared with two other influences which remain to be considered. These are: (1) the levy of tribute upon the masses for the direct profit of a few wealthy classes; and (2) the enormous taxation of the poor and almost entire exemption of the rich.

§ 15. **Protective taxes.** The first of these is not the most important; and it is one concerning which there is so much controversy, that it will be only briefly mentioned here. This is the tribute which a few rich men are enabled by this system to levy upon the rest of the community through so-called protective taxes upon competing products. The most moderate estimate of this item places it at three times the amount of duties actually collected by the government upon such products. As those who dispute this estimate assert that a protective tariff imposes no burden at all upon the people of the protected country, but that Europe pays all the protective taxes of America on European products, while America pays all the protective taxes of Europe on American products, there is no advantage in offering any compromise on this estimate. It may be taken as it is or rejected altogether. It is included in the computations hereafter given; but if rejected, it would not reduce the estimate of the effects of indirect taxation by so much as one half.

But the justice of allowing, in these calculations, for an addition to the cost of domestic productions to the consumer of fully three times the amount of all duties collected, is demonstrated in an appendix to the recent work of David A. Wells on *Economic Changes*, page 472. There can be no impropriety in saying that this appendix was not written by Mr. Wells, but is the work of a gentleman of unusual ability and experience in statistical fields, who is also much more conservative in his views than Mr. Wells. This appendix shows that the people of the United States have actually paid an average price for iron and steel, during ten years, ending in 1887, of $56,000,000 per annum in excesss of the average English price; while the official statistics show that the average revenue to the United States from duties on all iron and steel, during the same period, was less than $15,000,000 per annum. This shows an addition to the cost to the consumer of three and two thirds of the whole duty collected. But this is not all. Tin plates are included in the dutiable articles. No tin plates were produced here during those ten years; and therefore the increased cost of American production relates solely to other forms of iron products. Excluding these, the revenue from iron and steel has averaged less than $12,000,000 per annum, during the period referred to. The consumer has, therefore, paid over *four and one half times as much as the duty* in addition thereto.

§ 16. **Excise taxes.** The amount which should be allowed for the effect of internal taxes upon domestic production is much more difficult to estimate. That such taxes do increase the cost to the consumer, far in excess of the mere tax paid to the state, is very clear. The history of the match tax alone is sufficient to prove this. Levied solely for revenue, it soon ruined all small manufacturers and created a monopoly, which increased the price, not only by the one cent per box paid to the government, but by another cent; as was proved by the fact that the cost to consumers fell two cents soon after the repeal of the one-cent tax. And, for nearly two years after the tax was laid, this whole increase went into private pockets; the market being fully stocked, in anticipation of the tax. But it is not probable that all excise taxes operate quite so severely. Their influence in checking production, however, and the wholly unforeseen ways in which they hinder improvements and petrify industry, to the common loss, are well known. It would be a moderate estimate to put the indirect cost of such taxes at one fourth of the amount collected; but, having no proper basis for an estimate, it is better to make none.

§ 17. **Dealer's profits.** The profits of dealers upon the indirect taxes, which they pay in the first instance, are plainly a charge upon consumers. Take earthenware, as an example. In consequence of the great cost of handling these goods and the constant losses by breakage, the nominal profit of dealers is rarely as low as 50 per cent. This profit is charged, as a matter of course, upon the duty as well as upon the cost. The duty prior to 1894, was nominally 60 per cent., but actually nearer 70 per cent.; since packages are made dutiable, while they are useless, after being once used. To call the actual tax 66⅔ per cent. is moderate. But the tax to the consumer, plus the dealer's profit, was never less than 100 per cent. and often far more. Precisely the same addition would be made to the cost of a similar domestic article, if subject to a similar excise duty.

Nominal profits upon unbreakable articles are by no means so large. Yet to call the general average of mercantile profits, before the consumer is reached, only 15 per cent., is ridiculously low. No estimate, of which the writer is aware, puts it lower than 25 per cent. Nevertheless, the lowest conceivable figure shall be here accepted.

The profits collected upon local taxes on buildings and chattels must be put still lower. Let them stand at only 5 per cent.

§ 18. Burden of taxes and profits. On the basis of the foregoing explanations, and upon the census and other official statistics for 1880 (those for 1890 being not even yet quite complete), the following tables are constructed.

American Tax Burden of 1880.

Import duties	$186,500,000	
Internal revenue, etc.	147,000,000	
Increased prices domestic protected goods	559,500,000	
Total	$893,000,000	
Dealers' profits, 15 per cent.	134,000,000	
		$1,027,000,000
Local taxes	$312,000,000	
Landlords' and dealers' profits, 5 per cent	15,600,000	
		327,600,000
Grand total		$1,354,600,000

Out of what fund can these taxes and profits be paid? Not out of what the people spend, but out of what, but for these charges, they would save.

In proportion to what are they paid? Not in proportion to what is saved, but strictly in proportion to what is spent upon living. The larger the proportion which the necessary cost of mere subsistence for himself and his family bears to each man's income or property, the larger, in exact proportion, is his relative share of compulsory taxation. If he chooses, for his own pleasure, to increase his expenditure much beyond this limit, he bears a larger proportion of the actual burden of taxation; but this is not compulsory upon him.

As, however, nearly all men of more than average wealth do spend more than is absolutely necessary, the correct method of ascertaining the relative tax burden of each class is to estimate the average expenditure of that class, disregarding the extremes of extravagance or stint.

The estimate in Mr. Gannett's census report of accumulation for the ten years between 1870 and 1880 was $1,300,000,000 per annum. This figure will be accepted for the last year of the series. The census of 1890 estimates the annual savings since 1880 at $2,000,000,000.

§ 19. **Earnings of the people.** Adopting the census of 1880 as the basis, as we must at present, there were then about 17,400,000 producers, supporting each a group of three persons, disregarding fractions. The earnings of 3,000,000 to 5,000,000 farm laborers in the census year 1879 were shown by the agricultural report to be less than $194, on an average, including the cost of their living. The earnings of 4,000,000 farmers were less than $300 each. The earnings of 2,700,000 artisans averaged $346. It is often claimed that this represents only a portion of their earnings, and that the census gives the total amount of wages paid in the year against the largest number of laborers ever employed at any time. This is not true. The census distinctly states that only the average number of laborers is given; and therefore it is entirely proper that the whole amount of wages should be given. It is to be remembered that this average of $346 includes the earnings upon which a group of three only are supported. The average family numbering five, this income represents an average family income of $577. So far from being too low, this is actually much too high. It is much more than the average earnings of mechanics' families in cities. It is $62 more than the average railroad employee earned, in 1888, when working 313 full days in the year.[1] Four hundred and fifty dollars would be an ample estimate of the average income of four fifths of American families. Nevertheless, the excessive amount of $300 for each worker, equal to $500 for each family, will be here accepted as the lowest range of average income, with $400 for each worker, or $666 for each family, in the next grade.

What were the total earnings of the whole people? The officials, who had themselves taken a large part of the census of 1880, and who remained in office after General Walker retired, became alarmed at its showing upon this point. By no manipulation consistent with the figures could it be made to show a gross production of much more than $5,000,000,000 per annum. One census taker then guessed that farm products were underestimated $1,400,000,000, while another guessed that manufactures were underestimated $3,400,000,000. The agriculturist was not so wise as the manufacturer, and gave reasons for his guess. Of course the reasons cut down the guess at least one third. The manufacturing guess shows too much evidence of manufacture upon its face. Still, the real census figures are undoubtedly too low. We *have*

[1] *U. S. Labor Report*, 1889, p. 160.

to guess. Building up from the foundation of a minimum average earning of $300 for each worker, or $500 for each family (which is decidedly too much); allowing an average of $1,000 for each of 1,000,000 workers in the centre, which Mr. Atkinson has pretty clearly proved, and making the least reasonable allowance for the large incomes of the richer classes, we reach the conclusion that the actual production of the nation in 1880 was between $8,300,000,000 and $9,000,000,000. Prof. W. T. Harris, after analyzing the original and amended census figures, estimates the same income at only $7,300,000,000 (*Forum*, July, 1887). If the average income of the basic 13,000,000 workers was only $225 instead of $300, Professor Harris's estimate is probably correct. Knowing, as we do, that several millions of them did not average even $200, it is quite possible that he is correct. But as, upon this basis, the disproportion between the burdens imposed upon the rich and the poor would become too startling for general acceptance, it is better to err upon the safe side, and to assume that the earnings of farmers and mechanics were far greater than any one has ever been able to prove them to be. All such figures must necessarily be largely guesswork; but it will be found that no reasonable guesses can be made which will materially alter the final general result. We may proceed to rectify all these guesses, by comparison with actual returns of incomes, made during the existence of an income tax.

§ 20. **Income tax returns, 1866.** It is much to be regretted that no correct statistics of the incomes of the people of the United States, during the years when an income tax was levied, seem to be attainable. The figures given in Lalor's *Cyclopædia* do not agree in any respect with those of official reports of the Commissioners of Internal Revenue; and neither set of tables works out any result which agrees with the taxes collected. Only some suggestions towards a correct result can be gathered from any of these figures. It appears that in 1866, under a law exempting $600 and house rent, incomes were returned, from business profits and salaries, by 460,000 persons, to the gross amount of about $885,333,000; which, after adding the $600 exempted and an estimated average house rent of $400, which is none too much, would make a total income of $1,345,000,000. This amount represents that upon which the tax was paid in 1867; and, although a large part of this payment was made on account of assessments made in 1865, an equally large part of the assessments of 1866 was not paid until 1868; so that the one balances the other.

Of these 460,000 taxpayers, about 37,000 (or 8 per cent.) acknowledged incomes exceeding $5600 and house rent, which, in their cases, must be estimated at fully $900 additional. This would make their incomes exceed $6500. Their total incomes amounted to over $312,000,000, including house rent. This is somewhat less than 25 per cent. of the whole; but, as the proportion was much larger in 1865, 25 per cent. will be a fair average.

In the city of Brooklyn, in 1865, 1734 persons returned incomes exceeding $5600 and house rent; of whom 801 returned incomes exceeding $10,600 and rent. It will be reasonable to classify them into incomes of $6500 and of $12,500 minimum respectively. In the poorer district of Brooklyn, the richer class constituted 40 per cent. of the whole class above $6500; in the wealthier district, the proportion was 48 per cent. It will be a very moderate estimate to put the incomes of the whole country, exceeding $10,000, at $37\frac{1}{2}$ per cent. of all exceeding $5000. In Great Britain the proportion considerably exceeds 40 per cent.

Even in those European countries where the income-tax is most rigorously and honestly enforced, it is universally conceded that at least one third of the assessable income is never returned. In the United States there can be no doubt that less than half of the tax really due was ever collected. The administration of the law was everywhere corrupt; and in most of the western and southern States it was a mere farce. It is a moderate estimate to assume that there were really more than 800,000 persons in receipt of incomes exceeding $700, in 1866, and that their aggregate income exceeded $2,500,000,000, or about $3000 each on an average. These may be divided into three classes, viz.:

   I. 720,000 at $ 700 to $ 5,000.
   II. 50,000 " 5,000 " 10,000.
   III. 30,000 " over $10,000.

When the exemption was increased to $1000 and house rent, the number of taxpayers fell off to about 260,000; and upon the exemption of $2000 the number fell to 75,000. There is nothing to be learned from the study of returns so palpably fraudulent. It is to be hoped that much better information will be gathered from returns under the new law in 1895.

§ 21. **Estimated incomes, 1880.** The increase of wealth in the United States, between 1866 and 1880, according to the valuation of real estate (which is the only safe test), was 65 per cent. The increase of population was 35 per cent. Taking the medium figure of 50 per cent., as the increase in the number of large incomes, the result would be as follows:

American Incomes Over $700.

Incomes.	Persons.	
	1866	1880
$ 700 to $ 5,000	720,000	1,100,000
5,000 to 10,000	50,000	75,000
10,000 upwards	30,000	45,000
	800,000	1,220,000

We must collect any further light on the classification of incomes from a study of the British income-tax re-returns. The following table shows the official return of

GREAT BRITAIN AND IRELAND.
Business Incomes in 1884.

Persons.	Income.	Average Income.
104	£50,000 & over	£91,783
1,192	10 to 50,000	17,644
1,871	5 " 10,000	6,553
1,117	4 " 5,000	4,270
1,947	3 " 4,000	3,266
4,202	2 " 3,000	2,282
13,268	1 " 2,000	1,277
32,769	500 " 1,000 ⎫	541
19,996	400 " 500 ⎭	
48,572	300 " 400	367
110,626	200 " 300 ⎫	197
163,736	150 " 200 ⎭	
399,400		

These returns represent only earnings from personal services and profits derived from business, other than farming. Rents, incomes from corporate investments, mining, farming, etc., are not included. As 67,000 farmers and at least as many landlords also made returns, it is obvious that the list is a very incomplete statement of the income taxpayers. Not less than 200,000 British families live upon their investments alone; and the whole number of incomes above £150 must have exceeded 600,000 in 1884.

§ 22. **Savings of each class.** Let us now estimate the probable savings of each class, in 1880, after all taxes were paid.

Labor commissioners have repeatedly inquired into the savings of laborers, with the result of fixing these at not more than 5 per cent. of such incomes under $500, after all taxes have been paid. As taxes consume, directly and indirectly, at least 15 per cent. of a laborer's average income, the average laborer is not so thriftless as it might at first appear. He does not spend more than 80 per cent of his earnings. A paternal government takes care of that. The middle class find it difficult to save more than 10 per cent. But the savings of the rich proceed upon a rapidly increasing ratio, until we reach some men who save, with ease, 95 per cent. of their income. This is not common; but there are well-known instances of persons whose income exceeds $1,000,000, whose expenditures do not equal 2 per cent of their income. Such persons are practically exempt from all taxation by the Federal Government.

Constructing a table upon the foundations thus afforded, taking American statistics so far as they go, and using British statistics only for the purpose of supplementing and classifying American figures, the following is the result:

American Incomes, Expenses, and Savings, 1880.

Class.	Persons.	Income. Range.	Income. Average.	Average Expenses.	Average Savings.
I.	50	over $1,000,000	$1,500,000	$250,000	$1,250,000
II.	500	250,000 to 1,000,000	450,000	100,000	350,000
III.	5,000	50,000 to 250,000	88,000	40,000	48,000
IV.	12,500	20,000 to 50,000	27,500	15,000	12,500
V.	27,000	10,000 to 20,000	14,000	9,000	5,000
VI.	75,000	5,000 to 10,000	6,400	5,000	1,400
VII.	250,000	2,000 to 5,000	2,700	2,300	400
VIII.	850,000	700 to 2,000	1,000	850	150
IX.	2,500,000	350 to 700	400	380	20
X.	13,672,000	under 350	300	285	15

CROOKED TAXATION. 35

It is now necessary to tabulate the aggregate expenses and savings of each class, as an entire class.

American Incomes, Expenses, and Savings, 1880.

Class.	Persons.	Total Income.	Total Expenses.	Total Savings.
I.	50	$75,000,000	$12,500,000	$62,500,000
II.	500	225,000,000	50,000,000	175,000,000
III.	5,000	440,000,000	200,000,000	200,000,000
IV.	12,500	343,750,000	187,500,000	156,250,000
V.	27,000	378,000,000	243,000,000	135,000,000
VI.	75,000	480,000,000	375,000,000	105,000,000
VII.	250,000	675,000,000	575,000,000	100,000,000
VIII.	850,000	850,000,000	722,500,000	127,500,000
IX.	2,500,000	1,000,000,000	950,000,000	50,000,000
X.	13,672,000	4,101,600,000	3,896,520,000	205,080,000
	17,392,050	$8,568,350,000	$7,212,020,000	$1,356,330,000

§ 23. **Incidence of taxation.** The incidence of taxation is now to be considered. The gross expense of the people's living has been estimated, as above, at $7,212,000,000 for the year 1880. Taxation was distributed nearly pro rata upon this. The whole burden of taxation, including its intended and unintended effects, has been shown to be $1,350,000,000. This was equal to $18\frac{7}{10}$ per cent. on expenses. As the total savings, before taxes are deducted, would amount to $2,700,000,000, the ultimate burden imposed by taxation and its effects was 50 per cent. of all the national savings.

But, while this is the average, that average is based on a vast disproportion of burdens. The tax of $18\frac{7}{10}$ per cent. upon expenses means a tax of less than 4 per cent. upon the easy savings of the richest class, but of 78 per cent. upon the hard savings of the poorer class. Indirect taxation, therefore, bears twenty times as heavily upon the average poor man as it does upon the average rich man.

This will appear by the next table, in which is given:
1. The annual expenses of each class;
2. The tax burden at $18\frac{7}{10}$ per cent. on such expenses; and
3. The savings which each class could make, with no greater self-denial than at present, if it were relieved from all taxation.

American Tax Burdens, 1880.

rsons.	Total Income.	Expenses.	Tax Burden, $18\frac{7}{10}$ %.	Taxable Savings.	Saving after Ta
50	$75,000,000	$12,500,000	$2,337,500	$64,837,500	$62,...
500	225,000,000	50,000,000	9,350,000	184,350,000	175,...
5,000	440,000,000	200,000,000	37,400,000	277,400,000	240,...
12,500	343,750,000	187,500,000	35,062,500	191,312,500	156,...
27,000	378,000,000	243,000,000	45,441,000	180,441,000	135,...
75,000	480,000,000	375,000,000	70,125,000	175,125,000	105,...
50,000	675,000,000	575,000,000	107,525,000	207,525,000	100,...
50,000	850,000,000	722,500,000	135,107,500	262,607,500	127,...
00,000	1,000,000,000	950,000,000	177,650,000	227,650,000	50,...
72,000	4,101,600,000	3,896,520,000	728,649,240	933,729,240	205,...
92,050	$8,568,350,000	$7,212,020,000	$1,348,647,740	$2,704,977,740	$1,356,...

§ 24. **Concentration of wealth through unequal taxation.** The general effect of this inequality of taxation will be better understood by dividing the community into three classes, as is done in other countries, calling them the rich, the middle, and the laboring classes.

Under the system of taxation, existing in 1880, the stored-up wealth of the community was annually divided about as follows:

American Annual Accumulations, 1880.

Class.	Persons.	Accumulations.
Rich.	120,000	$873,750,000
Middle	1,100,000	227,500,000
Laboring	16,172,000	255,080,000
Total,	17,392,000	$1,356,330,000

If these calculations are at all correct, they demonstrate that, in 1880, fully half of the annual accumulations of the country fell into the hands of less than 28,000 families.[1]

But, it will be asked: Is this the result of indirect taxation? Certainly it is. If taxation were direct and exactly equal, the annual savings of each class should bear the same proportion to each other, after taxation, that they did before. Taxation, in short, should at least not make the poor relatively poorer than the richer classes. Let us see, then, how the case would stand if there were no taxes, no bounties, and no favoritism.

Natural Savings, in the Absence of Taxes, 1880.

Class.	Persons.	Untaxed Savings.
Rich.	120,000	$1,073,466,000
Middle.	1,100,000	470,132,500
Laboring.	16,172,000	1,161,379,240
Total,	17,392,000	$2,704,977,740

On this basis, it will be seen, the laboring masses would gain 43 per cent. of all the wealth, instead of less than 19 per cent., as at present; while the middle and laboring classes together would gain 60 per cent. instead of 36 per cent.

But upon what principle of equity or economic science should any artificial taxes be laid upon the masses of men, whose incomes fall below $400 to a family? Why should not taxation fall upon property instead of labor? Why should it be taken out of the means necessary to a bare living? It is idle to say that taxation of labor promotes economical government. It never has done so; and it

---

[1] Of the whole accumulation, $1,356,330,000, over $633,000,000 fell to 18,000 families, and $50,000,000 more to less than 10,000 families included in Class V.

never will. It has already been pointed out that indirect taxes are maintained for the very purpose of convincing the vast majority that they are *not* taxed, and that they have no interest in economical and prudent government. It is beyond contradiction that this is the design and effect of such taxes. It is absurd to contend that they must be maintained, in order to secure the votes of the majority for good and cheap government, when their chief object is to prevent these voters from feeling any personal interest in that question.

CHAPTER III.

DIRECT TAXATION.

§ 1. **Direct taxation practicable.** Nature having made it perfectly clear that indirect taxation is not natural, by making the collection of such taxes impossible without gross inequality, fraud, hindrance to production, and general demoralization, it is absolutely necessary for those who care for justice, equality, and good morals, to select some form of direct taxation.

The principal objection raised against direct taxation is the alleged unwillingness of the people to pay such taxes, and the consequent difficulty and expense of collecting them. So strongly is this objection felt, that many persons, who favor direct taxation for old-established communities, assume as an indisputable fact that, in new and thinly settled countries, it would be impossible to raise an adequate revenue by direct taxes.

As invariably happens, in cases where economic laws are thrust aside by practical men, on the plea that they are sound in theory, but will not work in practice, all human experience contradicts this assumption.

The newest and most thinly settled communities invariably do raise their public revenue by direct taxation; and indirect taxation is impossible, until they have obtained a considerable degree of growth and an advanced social organization. Can any society be more new or any country be more sparsely settled than were all the different territories of the United States, when first opened for settlement? Yet was there a single village or school district in them all, which raised its first revenues by indirect taxes? It may be said that this was only because the United States Constitution prohibited them from surrounding themselves with a tariff. But the history of mankind may be searched in vain for any absolutely new community, which raised its *first* taxes by means of a tariff on imports or on exports, by excise duties, or by any indirect taxes whatever. A moment's reflection will show that the very idea is absurd. Every new settlement is eager for imports; and it would rather offer a bounty for them than place a tax upon them. It clamors for production, manufactures, and trade; and it lays no taxes on production.

With this idea also falls the other idea, that direct taxes are necessarily more difficult of collection than others. *Some* forms of direct taxes are difficult of collection, and increasingly so as the community advances in wealth and civilization. This is because those particular taxes are not founded upon justice; and their injustice becomes more and more apparent with the growth of the community. But if it can be shown that there is a tax which men everywhere are willing to pay, partly because they feel that they receive full equivalent for the tax, and partly because the pressure for payment is practically irresistible, and if this tax can be collected with ease, equality, and justice, all these objections will fall to the ground.

As the only forms of direct taxation, now in use, by means of which an adequate public revenue could be obtained, are an Income Tax, a Succession Tax, and a tax upon the value of some part or all of real and personal property, usually called a General Property Tax, our attention may as well be confined to these taxes.

§ 2. **The general income tax.** The first impression of most students of taxation is probably in favor of a general income tax; that is, a tax upon incomes from earnings, as well as from investments. But this impression is soon dissipated by a careful study of the subject. Assuming this to be the only tax, it is manifestly unfair that a man who derives his income from accumulated wealth should pay no more than another, who earns all his income by hard personal labor. If the rate of taxation is uniform, it bears severely upon the poor, as compared with the rich. If it is graduated, increasing with increasing income, it cannot be efficiently collected; because the method of collection at the source of income, by authorizing corporations to deduct the tax from dividends and interest, and tenants to deduct the tax from their rents, would be im-. possible under a graduated tax; and the assessor would have no means of securing returns, except by the personal oath of the taxpayer, which long experience shows to be a very poor security. Under any system, an income tax upon earnings and profits has to be assessed largely in reliance upon such oaths; and the consequence is that, even under the rigid and honest administration of the law, which prevails in England and several European states, fully one third of this part of the tax is evaded by false returns. In the United States, during the ten years' existence of an income tax, the proportion of evasion was very much larger, averaging not less than half, for the entire period, and mounting up to more than two thirds at the close. In several States, there can be no doubt that nine tenths of the whole taxable income escaped from the tax. The general income tax is thus a fruitful source of perjury; and it cannot be a scientific or natural tax, for that reason. Since perjurers would thus escape taxation, in whole or in part, it is manifest that the tax would be unequal in its operation and would bear twice as heavily upon the honest as upon the dishonest.

Furthermore, a strict income tax would collect nothing from property which is held out of use. The landlord who improved his land would be taxed; but the landlord who held it vacant would not be taxed at all. Thus a bounty would be put upon land speculation. It may be said that the annual rise in value might be assessed as income. But it would not really be income; and a tax upon that would not be in fact or in law an income tax. If such fictitious incomes were assessed, every taxpayer must obviously be allowed to deduct from his income, for purposes of taxation, any fall in the value of his land, without testing the market by a sale. Such allowances, it is evident, would leave a wide door for fraud and evasion.

§ 3. **Excuse for income taxes in America.** Under the peculiar political conditions of the United States, there is much excuse for an income tax, as a transitionary measure of national taxation. The Federal Constitution requires all "direct taxes" to be apportioned among the States, according to population, with entire disregard of their wealth or land. A direct tax upon the value of real estate, under this provision, would exact from North Carolina about five dollars, and from South Carolina about seven dollars, on the same real-estate value which, in Rhode Island, would pay one dollar. It would exact from Missouri a larger tax than from Massachusetts and Rhode Island together; although the value of real estate in those two States is sixty per cent. greater than in Missouri. Each dollar's worth of land in Tennessee would be taxed more than twice as heavily as in Wisconsin. Taxes, even within New England, would be very unequally distributed. Land in Vermont would be taxed 150 per cent. more than in Massachusetts or Rhode Island. If personal property were also taxed, the discrepancies would be still greater.

Until April, 1895, it was supposed to be settled law that an income tax was not such a "direct tax," as the framers of the Constitution had in mind, and therefore that it could be levied without regard to population or State lines.[1] Decisions to this effect made this tax in effect the only direct tax, in the scientific sense, which could be adopted in the United States, without great inequalities between the States, until the Constitution can be amended. The recent judgment of the Supreme Court, exempting rents from income tax and casting doubt upon the whole system, will probably stir up a movement for such an amendment, which can easily be obtained, whenever the people are resolved to abolish all indirect taxation. But without the support of a very strong public sentiment, amendments to the Federal Constitution are impossible, as two thirds of Congress and three fourths of the State legislatures must concur in their adoption. The taxation of incomes in general, while rents are entirely untaxed, is a monstrous anomaly, which will certainly be remedied at a comparatively early day.

But as the purpose of the present inquiry is to ascertain what ought to be done, without regard to questions of present practicability or temporary expediency, this political difficulty need not be further discussed. It may be noted, nevertheless, that an income tax, levied exclusively at the sources of income, could be made to reach, with great approximation to equality, all rents, dividends, corporate payments of interest, and perhaps mortgage interest. As will be hereafter shown, the same results can

[1] Springer *v.* United States, 102 U. S., 586.

be attained by much better methods, so far as they ought to be attainable. But until the better method can be introduced, a tax upon incomes, at their source only, is much better than any form of indirect taxation. Only incomes from invested wealth can thus be reached (certain classes of salaries alone excepted); but no other incomes ought to be taxed.

§ 4. **Income tax unfitted for local use.** Even as a temporary expedient, however, the income tax, in any form, is entirely unfitted for use in American States and municipalities. New York, New Jersey, and Connecticut, for example, will never adopt an absolutely uniform income tax or administer it on uniform principles. The possessors of large incomes, therefore, would change their residences from one State or county to another, so as to make their returns wherever the law or the assessor was most favorable to them. If some States undertook to tax incomes at their source, while other States persisted in the old-fashioned method of individual returns of income received, there would be a great amount of double taxation. Rents of New York property, due to a Bostonian, would be taxed in New York against the tenant, and again taxed in Boston against the landlord. Such injustice would soon give provocation and excuse for fraudulent returns. There is an income tax in Massachusetts; but it is an utter failure, only aggravating the evils of the bad system of taxation there in use.

§ 5. **Other objections to income tax.** An income tax upon interest is clearly not a direct tax. The burden will be largely, if not entirely, shifted upon the borrower. A tax upon rents will fall principally upon what is not "rent" at all, in economic science, that is, upon the annual price paid for the use of buildings and improvements. All of this tax must, in the long run, be paid by the tenant. To this extent, therefore, it is an indirect tax; although not so easily shifted as are some other taxes. Upon the whole, not more than one third of any tax on incomes (other than earnings and profits) is strictly a direct tax.

The income tax can never be accepted as the only tax, for these and other reasons. It can be used only by national governments; and even in their hands it must be confined to subjects of taxation which can be much better reached by a straightforward tax upon values, instead of upon incomes. The general income tax, upon earnings and profits as well as upon fixed property, stands condemned by universal experience, as an incentive to perjury, a premium upon unproductive land, a special burden upon the honest, the simple, the widow, and the orphan. Nature shuts this door also in the face of honest men.

§ 6. **The succession tax.** The tax on successions, whether by legacy, devise, or inheritance, has lately become very popular. It is much more easily collected than the income tax, because it is paid by the administrators of dead men's estates, who have generally only a small interest in the estate, and whose conscience, if wounded by perjury, would not be soothed by the reflection that the profit was all their own. The ordinary human conscience becomes wonderfully tender, when asked to take a false oath for the benefit of some one else.

As a supplement to other taxes, the succession tax has been a fair success; because it has not become so heavy as to make living men willing to risk the loss of their property by schemes of evasion for the benefit of their heirs. But, if it became the sole method of taxation, it would be so heavy as to offer strong temptations to evasion. The highest estimate of the annual savings of the American people, added to the annual taxes, is not more than 22 per cent. of their annual earnings. The lowest estimate of their taxes is 7 per cent. of those earnings. As the value of property passing by succession in each year cannot, upon the average, exceed the annual savings, the succession tax, if it were the only tax, would absorb one third of all estates of deceased persons, even if every article of such estates passed through the probate courts and were fully taxed. This, however, we all know to be impossible. At the very least, one third of the property of descendants never did and never will go through the courts or be reached by any such tax. It is held in parcels so small as not to be worth the expense of court proceedings; and it consists of furniture, clothing, tools, money in hand, and other articles, which are readily disposed of by the family, without dispute or publicity. Therefore the tax actually levied upon such estates as would be reached by the assessors, if it were the only tax, would exceed 50 per cent. of their whole value.[1] Executors would be named from among legatees only; and this enormous tax would breed evasion and perjury among them, just as certainly as does the smaller tax, now imposed upon personal property by the several States. As such evasions increased, the tax upon the unfortunate few, who could not or would not obtain relief in the same way, would constantly increase, until the government would need 75 per cent. of all property reported; by which time the whole system would collapse. The succession tax may have some merits, considered as a mere supplement to other forms of taxation; but it never can be accepted as the one natural tax.

§ 7. **Succession tax oppressive on widows, etc.** There are other objections to this tax. If it is collected

---

[1] In New York, the local taxes alone exceed 40 per cent. of the value of property now reported for the succession tax.

impartially from all, it is obviously very severe in its operation upon widows, young orphans, and aged parents, who are the principal beneficiaries of dying persons. Just at the time when they are deprived of the earning power of the head of the family and are left with nothing but the income from his savings for their support —an income averaging less than one third or one fourth of that to which they were accustomed,—the State steps in and cuts off a large portion of this. From her that hath not, shall be taken even the little which she hath. If collected only or mainly from collateral relatives or strangers, such benefactions, which are often among the most commendable portions of a will, are sure to become more and more rare. It would thus greatly increase the tendency to concentration of wealth. If the succession tax were to become the only form of taxation, it would be impossible to make this distinction; because it would then absorb almost the whole of collateral inheritances, and no one, who had a wife or children, would leave a dollar to any one else. Even under a very moderate tax it was speedily found, in the State of New York, that legacies to benevolent and philanthropic institutions were discouraged; and the legislature has exempted them from much of this taxation.

§ 8. **Succession tax leads to public waste.** Another objection to the succession tax, as a principal source of revenue, and one which ought to be conclusive against its adoption as the *only* source, is that it must be constantly maintained at about one uniform rate. It cannot be frequently changed without gross injustice. If it fluctuates according to the needs of government, the estate of one man, who died on December 31st, might be taxed twice as much as the estate of another, who died on January 1st. Wherever this tax exists, it is always maintained at the same rate for a long series of years. If it were the only tax, it is obvious that it must be kept at a rate which would *always* produce a surplus revenue; for if it were not, it would often fall below the needs of government. It would therefore always lead to public extravagance and corruption. But even where it is only one of several taxes, as in the State of New York, experience already shows that it has the same effect, in a less degree. While at first it reduces the burden of other taxation, it soon tempts the government to increase expenditures to a point which will require as much other taxation as the people were accustomed to before. Accordingly, there has been a notable increase in the expenses of government in States which have an efficient succession tax; while the taxpayers are hoodwinked by a pretended reduction of their burdens.

CHAPTER IV.

TAXATION OF PERSONAL PROPERTY.

§ 1. **General property tax.** The first natural impulse of most men, when called upon to devise a system of direct taxation, is to propose a general property tax, that is, to make a valuation of all property, of every kind, and to tax every man in precise proportion to his share of the general wealth. Our law divides property into two classes, real and personal, or, as the civil law describes them, movable and immovable. The difference between the two species of property is so great, especially when considered with reference to taxability, that we must separately discuss the proposed taxation of personal property.

In every State of this Union the attempt is made to tax personal property, as well as real, by a direct tax upon its appraised value. In many States this attempt is sustained by stringent legislation; in some by the use of arbitrary and despotic powers. In other States the laws are crude, loose, and easily evaded. In all, there is a clamorous popular demand for more stringent legislation, in support of which farmers, especially, are almost unanimous.

Before inquiring into the testimony of experience as to the practicability and effects of such taxation, let us consider what is to be said from the theoretic point of view. What is personal property? Is it desirable, in the interest of the whole community, that all or any of it should be taxed? Does reason indicate that it can be fairly and equally taxed?

§ 2. Taxation of credits. Personal property may be divided into two classes: chattels and credits. Under the name of credits are to be included, not only book accounts, bills, notes, bonds, mortgages, bank deposits, and the like, but also shares of corporate stock, and probably shares in any partnership. "Our" chattels, properly speaking, are only those things which we have in our immediate custody; but chattels on special deposit may be included, since they are in the custody of our agents, who have no right to use them, even for a moment, for their own purposes.

Even including chattels held in partnership, in the class of strict chattels, it is universally admitted that, in all civilized countries, credits form by far the larger portion of personal property. It is easy to see why this is so. Credit may be given for more than two thirds of the value of both chattels and real estate, and it is continuously given to the extent of at least half the value of both. Prof. H. D. McLeod maintains, with tremendous energy and some ferocity, that the wealth of the community is actually increased by credits, to their full amount. This is a doctrine dear to the farmer's heart, as justifying all his favorite theories of taxation. It can be easily tested. It would be quite possible to form a syndicate in this country, owning property readily salable for two billion dollars. Let the syndicate mortgage this property for half its market value. That will add one billion to the national wealth. As loans might safely be made upon this mortgage to its full face value, let A, the first lender, hypothecate it as security for another loan of a billion, and B pledge it again to C, C to D, D to E, and so on, until promissory notes are outstanding to the amount of sixty billions, all secured by the original mortgage for one billion. All this, on the farmer's theory, is an actual increase of national wealth, for every note is perfectly good. The wealth of the United States is doubled in one day. The philosopher's stone and Fortunatus' purse are completely outdone.

But why confine ourselves to paper promises? Is not our word as good as our bond? There are more than ten million men in the United States accustomed to business of some kind. Let each of them agree to pay to his next neighbor one million dollars. No writing is necessary. The promise of No. 1 to pay No. 2 will be good, because founded upon the promise of No. 10,000,000 to pay the same amount to No. 1. It will cost them nothing, because all their promises can be literally fulfilled, without using a dollar. But (on the McLeod-farmer-credit tax theory) the United States will increase its wealth by the gigantic sum of ten million million dollars ($10,000,000,-000,000), all in talk. How little knew the ancient sage, who said: "The talk of the lips tendeth only to penury." (Proverbs, xiv., 23.)

§ 3. **Debt cannot increase wealth.** But what says plain common-sense? Debt cannot increase the general stock of wealth. Every credit implies a debit. One gives exactly as much as the other gets. A loan, secured by the pledge of a chattel, divides the equitable title to that chattel between the borrower and the lender, giving to the lender the meat and leaving to the borrower whatever may cling to the bone. The mortgage of land, at common law, transferred the actual ownership of the land to the mortgagee; and although equity has nominally altered this rule, the bottom fact is that the mortgagee still has the best half of the ownership. He is the real owner of the land, to the extent of his loan; although he can only enforce his ownership through a sale of the land. Or, to put it in another form, the title is divided between the mortgagor and the mortgagee: the mortgagee having the cream and the mortgagor the skimmed milk.

The same thing is true concerning every form of debt. Notes (unsecured by pledge or mortgage), book accounts, and debts of every kind are of no value whatever, except so far as they constitute a good and readily enforceable claim against equivalent visible, tangible things in the hands of the debtors. And to this extent the property in the hands of the debtor really belongs to the creditor; although the latter has no right to select any particular article or to seize anything, until his debt is due. If the debt stands against no tangible property, it is worthless; and, even under the McLeod theory, it would add nothing to the general wealth. If it does stand against such property, it diminishes the general stock just as much, by its lien on that property, as it adds by its own face value; and therefore it still adds nothing to the general wealth.

It may be asked: "Is not wealth in fact greatly increased by credit? Does not wealth grow more rapidly in a country where credit is freely given, than in one where no man will lend anything?"

Certainly. But only because credit is the instrument by which capital is transferred, for a time, from the hands of the men who cannot use it most productively, into hands of men who can. The gain in general wealth consists only in the difference between what such capital will produce in the hands of the borrower and what it would have produced in the hands of the lender.

§ 4. **Taxation of credit a useless labor.** Considered from the tax collector's point of view, it may be conceded that, as he has a definite sum to collect, the total burden of taxation will neither be increased nor diminished by any duplication or omission of wealth. It may, therefore, be further conceded that, if all forms of credits could be effectually reached and taxed, the tax would simply be divided among those who divide the ownership of things, and so no injustice would be done. Assuming, for the moment, that any form of personal property ought to be taxed, it may also be assumed that the double taxation involved in taxing credits would do no harm, *if they could all be reached.*

On the other hand, what advantage is there in doing this, if it can be done? Why take the trouble to collect taxes from two, three, or four persons on account of one piece of property? It increases the cost of collection without the slightest benefit to the State; and it confers no benefit upon the taxpayers. " The borrower is servant to the lender." He must eventually repay whatever tax the lender may be compelled to pay upon the loan, if the tax is impartially laid and fully collected, as we are now assuming that it can and will be.

§ 5. **Taxation of corporate credits.** But it is now time to inquire (still upon theoretic grounds) whether it is possible to collect taxes upon credits impartially and fully, or even to approximate such a result. It would seem possible to ascertain the amount and value of the stock and bonds of domestic corporations, especially of railway companies; because they can be compelled to make a full disclosure of their affairs; they must keep regular and full books of accounts; and their officers have not usually such an overwhelming interest in their finances as to make them willing to run great risks, merely for the sake of evading corporate taxation. This is far too liberal a concession; because immense blocks of shares are now owned by individuals, who either personally manage the corporations in which they are interested, or would make it a condition of the appointment of managers that they should commit whatever amount of perjury could prudently be used for the purpose of evading taxes. It is idle to say that managers of such easy consciences will not be trusted with the administration of great affairs. It is notorious that bribery, upon the most extended scale, is practised by the managers of some corporations, conducted otherwise with more than ordinary integrity; and we are all familiar with the story, undoubtedly true in substance, of the railway president who told all the other members of a presidents' conference that he would take the word of any of them, as a gentleman, for a million dollars, but as a railway officer, not for a cent.

Assuming, however, that the direct taxation of corporations could be successfully enforced, this could only be done in those States in which their business is and must be carried on. The stock and bonds of a New Jersey corporation are often owned entirely in New York; but in nearly all cases they can only be taxed in New Jersey. If the corporate property is situated in New Jersey, the same result would be secured by taxing the property itself. If that is done, the stock and bonds should be exempted; or, if they are taxed, the visible chattels and real estate of the corporation should be exempted. Is not the natural and sensible method to tax *things* and exempt *stock?*

The Federal Constitution stands in the way of taxing corporate bonds, by confining local taxation to bonds held by citizens or residents of the taxing State.[1] If such taxation became heavy, it would soon be found that all bonds were held outside of the State in which the corporate office was situated.

---

[1] Foreign-held Bonds, 15 Wallace, 300.

The ingenuity of corporations in evading taxation, even now, is well known. Is it supposable that, under a much heavier rate of taxation, such as must follow the abolition of all indirect taxation, this ingenuity would fail to put corporations upon an equal footing with individuals? If it did fail, the burden would become so heavy that the number of corporations would rapidly diminish; and the revenue from this source would fall off accordingly.

§ 6. **Taxation of individual credits.** Turning now to the case of individuals, it is certain that a very large majority keep no detailed account of their property or income, and that a majority of those who do would cease to do so, if by that means only they could avoid excessive taxation. Let us therefore inquire how heavy the general property tax would probably be, if there were no other taxes.

Assuming that property to the nominal value of $250 and the real value of $500 would be exempt, as it certainly would, and that all citizens handed in true lists of their property, as they certainly would not, not more than 2,500,000 of the 12,500,000 families in the United States would have personal property of sufficient value to subject them to direct taxation. Reckoning the total wealth of the country at $60,000,000,000, including the value of land, but allowing for inevitable exemptions in favor of poverty, of public property, charities, etc., and for the low rates at which property must always be assessed (say, at the utmost, 80 per cent. of its full value), the most honest and rigid assessment would fail to reach more than $40,000,000,000 of property.

As the federal and local taxes together exceed $850,000,000 per annum, the general property tax, if adopted as the only tax, would exceed 2 per cent. upon capital, even if there were no considerable evasion of taxes. This would be equivalent to a tax of more than one third of the income of all capital.

Call the tax only one third of the income from capital; and would not such a rate offer ample inducement for evasion? It has been found by experience that half this rate has sufficed to drive several hundred millions of wealth out of Boston and other cities; while under a two per cent. rate in New York, personal property has become almost invisible. It is manifest that practically all owners of credits would use their utmost efforts to conceal them from the assessor. Those who would not take a false oath would simply make no returns, submitting to any arbitrary tax which might be imposed upon them. Others would, in the vast majority of cases, make a false return. Some, knowing that the assessor would not believe them, if they denied the possession of any credits, would admit a part of their holdings; others would deny them altogether.

Thus the amount of taxable property discovered by the assessor would be further decreased; and, as the same amount of taxes must still be collected, the rate would rise to 3 per cent. This would make it simply impossible for strictly honest persons to hold credits at all, unless by their gradual withdrawal from the loan market the rate of interest should be increased to an amount equal to the additional tax. The more probable result would be to throw all such securities into the hands of less scrupulous persons; who, partly by a free use of perjury, and partly by an outward show of poverty, would blind the eyes of the most incorruptible assessors. Add to all this the possibility of corruptible assessors; and the field for evasion is enormously extended.

We may therefore safely conclude that by far the larger part of all credits would escape from taxation, that strictly honest holders would pay an outrageously disproportionate share of the taxes, the timidly dishonest or highly ingenious a moderate tax, and the utterly unscrupulous practically none at all.

§ 7. **Taxation of money.** Money, which is the one thing above all others which farmers desire to tax, is the very thing which, above all others, ought not to be taxed. A really effective and uniform system of taxing money would ruin every farmer in the country.

Money is as important to the prosperity of the community as blood is to the life of the individual. Taxation tends to drive money out of the State ; and, if any successful method of taxing all coin and other money could be put in operation, *all* money would be driven out of circulation ; and a frightful prostration of business would ensue; in which none would suffer more than the farmers. Farmers always want to get high prices for their products; and no more effective scheme could be devised for cutting down the prices of those products to the lowest point, than a tax which should really reach every dollar of money in the State.

Under the name of money, legislatures seek to tax:

1. Deposits in banks ;
2. Treasury notes and bank notes;
3. Gold and silver coins.

§ 8. **Bank deposits.** Bank deposits are not money, in any sense whatever. Nobody owns any money on deposit, unless it is a special deposit, in a separate bag or box. No bank accepts such a deposit, unless it is well paid for the trouble and risk. That is the business of safe-deposit companies ; it is no part of a banking business. Bank deposits are mere credits, like any other loan, payable on demand. No bank ever keeps on hand an amount of coin or notes equal to its deposits; which proves that the depositors cannot possibly have "*money* on deposit," since the money is never there to be had. Every reason for not taxing credits applies to bank deposits. But in addition to those reasons, success in taxing deposits would destroy the whole banking system and paralyze commerce, by compelling all exchanges to be settled in coin or bank notes, which are entirely insufficient for one tenth of commercial transactions.

§ 9. **Paper money.** So far as what is called money consists of paper, it is very clear that all this paper is mere evidence of debt. Treasury notes represent a debt of the United States; and bank notes represent debts of the banks. If the property which is represented by these notes is taxed, it ought not to be taxed a second time by taxing the notes themselves. If that property is *not* taxed, this only proves that the legislature, with the strongest desire to do so, has never been able to invent any method by which it could tax visible property; and if the legislature is not able to find and tax the houses, merchandise, food, and furniture, against which these notes were issued, these being things which cannot be put out of sight, how absurd it is to try to tax the notes themselves, which can so easily be put out of sight.

§ 10. **Coin.** Coin, like all other money, is nothing but a representative of wealth, an order for wealth, which everybody honors; but not wealth itself.

Gold or silver *coin* is of no earthly use, except for the purpose of exchanging one kind of merchandise for another. Nobody can eat coins, or wear coins, or build a house with coins, or even make a piece of plate with coins, or, in short, put them to any use of any kind whatever, *so long as he keeps them in coin.* The only purpose for which money is good at all is the purpose of getting rid of it, as quickly as possible, for something more practically useful. Accordingly, no man, who is not partially insane, habitually carries any large amount of money with him, or keeps it in his house. The very richest men have the least amount of money. A well-known citizen of New York, who is reputed to be worth $50,000,000, never possesses so much as $5 in actual money, if he can help it. He is supposed to have a large amount of money in banks, but he does not have a dollar of his own in any bank. All which he has is the promise of banks to pay a large sum to him, whenever he wants it; but, as a matter of fact, he never does want it, for his own personal use, and never takes possession of it. He only orders it to be paid to other people.

These views are supported by the Ohio Tax Commission of 1893. They say: "As to money, there is much reason for saying it is a mere tool, and that it should not be taxed at all. . . . Money is, after all, in almost all of its forms, a mere credit."[1]

It is a striking illustration of the total failure of reasoning power, in a majority of intelligent human beings, that the popular demand for more rigid taxation of money proceeds exclusively from that class of the people (mostly farmers and their associates) who at the same time most clamorously demand the issue of more money. Millions of voters demand, in the same breath, that money shall be issued in such quantities as to reduce the rate of interest to 2 per cent. and that the same money shall be taxed 2½ per cent. More than this, they insist that the men to whom they give their promissory notes for money lent shall be taxed 2½ per cent. on the notes, while they themselves shall be taxed 2½ per cent. on the money. In short, they want the price of money reduced to 2 per cent. and

[1] *Report Ohio Com.*, p. 65.

yet to bear a tax of 5 per cent. Thus the State would, if they could have their way, collect $5 out of every $2; an income tax of 250 per cent.

§ 11. **Taxation of banks.** The capital of incorporated banks is the one brilliant exception to the general failure of the personal-property tax. After many unsuccessful experiments, the State authorities finally devised a plan for taxing the shareholders of such capital, upon the value of their shares; and this tax is fairly assessed and effectually collected, with certain exceptions not necessary to be stated. The essential features of this plan are that the tax is laid upon the shareholders, not upon the banks, while it is paid by the banks and collected by them from the shareholders. Incorporated banks are always subject to rigid governmental inspection; and therefore it is impossible for them entirely to conceal the value of their assets from the government. Their entire business depends upon their credit; and their credit cannot be sustained without regular public reports of their financial condition. Thus the value of their stock is a matter of general knowledge; and, as a rule, it is estimated too high rather than too low. If, for the sake of evading taxation, the officers of a bank should contrive to depreciate the nominal market value of its stock, they would certainly lose more business than the saving of taxes would be worth, and they might lose their clientage altogether.

Banks are thus more effectively taxed than any other form of personal property. But is the result profitable to the people who lay the taxes? A little reflection will show that it is singularly disastrous. The success of the tax on banks is the chief source of American currency troubles.

§ 12. **The currency problem.** The widespread demand for more currency, which is so often treated with contempt by financiers, is at its foundation perfectly reasonable and natural; although every form of relief, which has thus far been demanded, would be ineffectual; while all that has thus far been done, in compliance with this demand, has brought ruin, instead of relief. The greenback craze, the demand for "free banking," meaning only the unlimited issue of bank notes, the silver mania, the 2 per cent. sub-treasury scheme, and all other proposals for an enormous expansion of the currency, arise from a common and permanent cause. The uneducated masses are not to be condemned for seeking relief in wrong directions, so long as the educated classes do not offer relief in any direction.

It is perfectly true, as alleged by the advocates of inflation, that there is not money enough to do the business of the country. But it is also true that *there never can be money enough to do the business of the country*. It can no more be done with fifty dollars per capita than with five. It must be done by barter, by book accounts, or by banking. As a matter of fact, it is done by a species of banking. But the banks of the South and Southwest are mainly cross-road grocery stores. Here, nine tenths of the farmers' and planters' produce are settled for. No matter to whom the products are sold, the producers get their pay only in trade at the village grocery. The process is as truly one of banking as is any transaction in a national bank of New York or Chicago. But it is enormously expensive, clumsy, risky, and unsatisfactory. Precisely the same transaction which, in a large city, would cost the farmer less than $2\frac{1}{2}$ per cent., costs him, at his village store, 20 to 25 per cent. Yet the clumsiness of the village transaction is so great that the storekeeper does not, in the long run, make any remarkable profit from this enormous commission.

Why is this? Because there are no regular banks, within the reach of the farmer. But why are there no such banks? Simply because the farmer himself has taxed them out of existence. Or, more accurately, because his beloved system of taxation has made it impossible for good banks to come into existence in his neighborhood. The real business of a bank is to enable goods to be exchanged, without the use of any money. Issuing notes is not at all essential to a banking business. But the strictly regular business of a bank cannot be carried on, in a purely farming district, under the burden of local taxation. There is not enough profit in it to pay the tax. In Canada and Scotland, where banks pay no local taxes, every little village has a branch bank, supported by the wealthy bank of some large city. In the United States, where all banks are heavily taxed, there are not one fifth of the number necessary to supply the demand; and as no branches are allowed, most of the country banks are not thoroughly safe. In Canada and Scotland there is no currency question. Nobody wants greenbacks or sub-treasuries, or cares anything about bimetallism. In the United States we hardly think about anything else.

The moral is plain. Abolish taxation on personal property, including all taxes on banks, allow branch banks to be set up everywhere, and the currency question will settle itself.

§ 13. **Taxation of visible chattels.** Some writers on the subject, who fully admit that invisible and intangible personal property ought not to be taxed, nevertheless insist that everything should be taxed, which can be seen and touched. They see clearly that mortgages represent real estate; that promissory notes and book-debts represent the cloth, groceries, metals, or the like, for which they are given; that the stock of a railway company represents the railway and its equipment, and that there is no sense or justice in taxing both the things which are represented and the pieces of paper which represent them. They see, too, that bonds, notes, and money can be hidden, and that any attempts to tax them must result in doubling the burden of simplicity and honesty and exempting shrewdness and roguery. But they insist that all such personal property as can be seen and handled, and cannot easily be concealed, ought to bear its share of taxation, and that it can be reached, effectually and equally.

Let us first consider what articles of personal property can be seen and touched, so as to be reached by faithful assessors. The results of actual assessments, in States which adopt stringent methods of personal taxation, show that these " visible and tangible things " are principally animals, stock on hand of merchants and manufacturers, household furniture, farm implements and carriages, in the order named. As the only reason for taxing these things, while letting invisible property pass, is that the assessment of invisible property must depend upon the oath of the taxpayer, we must inquire how far these visible articles can be fairly reached and valued by assessors, without depending upon the statements of their owners.

§ 14. **Farmers hold most visible chattels.** Judged by this standard, it is manifest that the property of farmers would be more easily reached and more accurately valued by honest assessors, than would be the property of any other class. For farm animals and implements are always readily open to inspection. Their value is generally nearly uniform. Most farmers, in the same county, pay about the same prices for their horses, cattle, plows, tools, and furniture. A few own highly expensive cattle; and these will escape full assessment, just as other chattels of very rich people will, in any line of business. But the mass of farmers own things which their neighbors can value easily. Very different is the case of merchants. What assessor, however honest and competent, can personally value all the stock of even one grocery store, not to say the stock of all the stores in his district? Fancy an assessor making a personal appraisal of the stock of fifty drug stores, a hundred dry-goods stores and as many grocery stores. In every large store, there are hundreds of different articles, at different prices, by the yard or the pound or the gallon. Bales of goods lie side by side; some worth four cents a yard, some ten cents, some two dollars. The difference between goods worth one dollar a yard and those worth two dollars is often imperceptible to the eye of any one but an expert. But how can an assessor have time to open all these bales, to look at them, much less judge accurately of their value? All the assessors of New York City could not approximately value Claflin's stock alone, without relying upon the word of Claflin's clerks. Therefore the stock of merchants and manufacturers would be assessed upon the valuation given by themselves; as, in fact, it is now. Thus the assessment of "visible and tangible property," in these important cases, is made and must be made in exactly the same manner as the assessment of bonds, notes, and other invisible property, resulting in a double or treble burden upon the simple and truthful, as compared with their unscrupulous neighbors.

The same thing is true as to household furniture. Farmers have a certain average quality of furniture, the value of which can be ascertained far more nearly than the value of that of well-to-do city residents. In proportion to the wealth of the taxpayer, would be the failure of the most honest assessor to estimate the true value of his property. Anybody can estimate the value of a two-dollar chair; but few indeed can tell the difference between a chair costing fifty dollars and another costing one hundred and fifty. To many assessors there would be no apparent difference in value; to none would the fair difference seem to be more than twenty dollars or thereabouts. In many household articles, such as bedding, for example, a difference of 200 per cent. in cost is attended with no outside indications. Many honest assessors would reckon the value of a $15,000 set of furniture as no greater than that of a set costing less than half the price.

§ 15. **Assessment of merchandise.** Let us, however, imagine a sustained and general attempt to appraise visible chattels by public officers. How can that vast mass of visible chattels, known under the general name of merchandise, and which is obviously that which the advocates of chattel taxation are most anxious to reach, be fairly, equally, and effectually taxed? In the first place, they must be appraised, all over the United States, on the same day. Merchandise is constantly changing its ownership and constantly changing its situation. A bale of cloth, for example, manufactured in Lowell, is sent, unbroken, to New York, and there divided among buyers from Cleveland, Indianapolis, Chicago, Milwaukee, Minneapolis, Des Moines, Omaha, and Denver. Thus the title to this one parcel of goods passes through ten different owners, residing in ten different States, each of which has its own appointed day of assessment for purposes of taxation. Under a system of assessment, executed by public officials, without depending upon the false returns of interested taxpayers, it would certainly happen, in many cases, that the cloth would be taxed once in Lowell, taxed again in New York, taxed again in each of the cities to which it was next sold, and taxed once more in the retail stores of the country districts where it would be finally sold for actual use. This would make four taxes upon one thing. Side by side with cloth thus taxed will be found other cloth, of precisely the same quality and make, which had luckily been started on its way from Lowell before Lowell's assessment day, slipped through New York and Chicago before their assessment days, and finally received by the country dealer just after his assessment day. At the present average rate of taxation, the country dealer who was clever enough thus to escape the various local taxes would have an advantage of 8 or 10 per cent. over his less ingenious neighbor. All dealers who paid the tax on their goods would thus be driven out of business by the competition of those who did not.

§ 16. **Work for assessment day.** Let us imagine, then, that the States all agree upon one day for assessment. The first of April, which is the day selected in some places, is decidedly the most appropriate day for this purpose. On that day, all over the country, a swarm of assessors must besiege the factories, mills, shops, and stores, taking an honest valuation of all merchandise on hand. The valuation must be completed in one day. Otherwise, Smith's valuation being completed on April 1st, while Jones is left to April 2d, there would be a midnight exodus of easily portable goods from Jones to Smith, so that the assessor should find little value in charge of Jones on April 2d. No help must be asked in the work of valuation from the owners or their employees; for if that is done, the assessor might just as well accept the sworn returns of the owners, as is done now, with most ludicrous and iniquitous results. As it is well known to be an impossibility for the owners themselves to make such a valuation in one day, even with the aid of all their clerks, there must be a number of official assessors employed, exceeding all the number of persons employed in holding and selling merchandise. The work might, however, by extreme diligence, be done in a rough way by two million local assessors. As it would take them at least one day to receive instructions and two days to tabulate their returns, besides the one day occupied in valuing, each would serve at the very least for four days. If they were paid less than $5 per day, on an average, their services would be worthless. The lowest cost of such an assessment would therefore be $40,000,000.

§ 17. **Vanishing merchandise.** On "assessment day" there would be universal concealment of all articles of small bulk and great value. Watches, jewels, gold, money of all kinds, and all concealable things would vanish from sight. Men would walk about stuffed with valuables. Old stoves, pots, and pans would be filled with money and jewels. Valuable goods, which could not be hidden, would be covered with dust or otherwise made to look almost worthless. In every mill and factory manufactures would be kept in an unfinished state, as far as possible, until assessment day had passed. A thousand devices would be resorted to, in order to reduce the apparent value of the things which the assessor would inspect, or to prevent him from seeing them at all.

In order to make this plan of official valuations successful, the assessors must enter every room in every house, and strip naked every man and woman whom they suspect of concealing taxable property. This is the method by which tariffs on imports are executed; and it is the only way in which visible, tangible personal property ever was or ever can be fairly, equally, and effectually taxed.

Americans, boasting loudly of their freedom and personal dignity, do submit to all these outrages, under the tariff and excise system; and only a few moonshiners in Southern States resent them. The whole system of indirect taxation is enforced by the violation of all privacy, decency, and natural rights. Everybody is presumed, by our tariff and excise laws, to be a thief and a liar; and everybody who comes under the operation of those laws is actually treated as such. But, meek and spiritless as the residents of American cities have shown themselves under corrupt and brutal police, and indifferent as all Americans have shown themselves to innumerable forms of plunder, carried on under the pretense of collecting indirect taxes, is it probable that they would submit to the universal application of these methods, under direct local taxation? Would they long submit to have their beds searched for concealed money and their wives stripped to discover concealed jewelry, as is now done by customhouse officers?

And, when all this was done, the system would none the less fail. The official valuation of visible chattels could not be completed within ten days; and it would therefore be successfully evaded. It could not be made even approximately correct. Every article would be valued very much too high or very much too low. Nor would the average produce any fair result. The goods of Jones would be appraised at twice their real value; while the goods of Smith would be appraised at nearly their value, and the goods of Brown at half their value. Jones would thus be cheated heavily, Smith moderately, for the sole benefit of Brown.

The fact is that all systems of assessing personal property are about equally bad. Probably the nearest approach to a fair assessment would be reached by requiring every citizen to make a return for his next neighbor.

Such a system would be as absurd as an old-fashioned donkey race, in which each man rides a competitor's donkey, and the last donkey wins. But, like such a race, it might work out rough justice—*very* rough, it is true, but not so bad as the results of any system now in use.[1]

[1] While these pages were going to press, the writer discovered that this very method had been tried in Rhode Island, a hundred years ago, with only the difference that each assessment was to be made by *ten* neighbors. And the Romans (A.D. 300–800) had an even more effective plan. *They compelled the assessor to pay all the taxes which could not be collected from his neighbors!* And yet both Rome and Rhode Island failed to make their systems work.

CHAPTER V.

TESTIMONY OF EXPERIENCE.

§ 1. **Personalty taxes in history.** It is time to test these theories by actual experience. European governments, for several centuries, persisted in the effort to appraise and tax all classes of property, real and personal, upon an equal footing. The ancient tax-rolls of England enumerate the precise number and value of the beds, tables, chairs, pots, and pans of each taxpayer.[1] The English tax, now called the land tax, imposed in the seventeenth century, was in fact originally a tax upon all real and personal property. As late as 1827, a trifling amount of personal property was assessed and taxed under this law. The only reason why such property dropped out of the assessment rolls was that it became increasingly impossible to reach it. Practically, it dropped out at a very early day. A similar experience in all Europe led to similar results; and the attempt to assess personal property, whether visible or invisible, otherwise than by means of an income tax, has been universally abandoned.

But the citizens of our own favored land, confident in the power of the American eagle and of republican institutions, despise the teachings of European experience and resolutely persist in the taxation of personal property. They have achieved a certain measure of success. The official assessors estimate that they have reached nearly

[1] Dowell's *Hist. Taxation*, 59-74; 232-235.

60 per cent. of such property in New England, 50 per cent. in some Western States and 15 per cent. in New York. If by "personal property" only visible chattels were intended, this estimate may be correct. But as this is not intended, the estimate is excessive. In no large State does the assessed value of personal property materially exceed half the assessed value of real estate, or amount to one third of its actual value. In some States (Alabama, for example) the roll of personalty is swelled by including in it all railway values. But it is everywhere conceded that personalty, if defined as including all forms of liens and loans, fully equals realty in value. It would be strange if it did not; because such a definition includes all chattels, all debts incurred in the purchase of chattels, and all debts which are made a charge upon land. This is the value which our legislators strive to tax; and it would be too liberal to allow that they reach one third of it anywhere.

Long study of all accessible statistics has convinced the writer that the average market value of improved land, irrespective of improvements, is almost exactly equal to the value of all improvements affixed to it, that the value of actual visible chattels is about the same, and that the value of unimproved land is about half as much. In other words, dividing salable property into seven equal parts, land would represent three sevenths, improvements on land two sevenths and chattels two sevenths. This appears to be the fact in every civilized country; and the reason, in part, may be readily discerned. The "value of land" consists of nothing whatever, except a power of exacting tribute from labor by means of ground rents.[1]

[1] This has just been adjudged by the U. S. Supreme Court (Pollock v. Farmers' Loan Co., April, 1895). As a scientific question, it was never open to doubt.

The fruits of labor, in which alone this tribute can be paid, consist solely of improvements and chattels. It is impossible that the value of land should exceed the other values combined; because that would mean that landlords got more than there is to get. In the struggle between the landlord, the capitalist, and laborer, we might reasonably anticipate that the landlord would not get more than one third of the whole net produce; and this appears to be the actual average. Vacant land brings no present rent; but it has a market value equal to the present value of its expected future rent. And this is of course an additional value in the landlord's possession.

But nowhere are actual chattels found by assessors to anything like this proportion of the value of land. Taking only places in which there are rigid assessment laws, rigidly enforced, Boston discovers visible chattels to the amount of only 2½ per cent. of its real estate, Cincinnati to only 10 per cent., Ohio to only 15 per cent., Minnesota to only 20 per cent.; whereas, in each case, the proportion should be 40 per cent. Here, as in every other instance, it is noticeable that the proportion of chattels discovered by the assessor is greater and greater as the proportion of farmers to the entire population increases.

§ 2. **Taxation of personal property always a failure.** If anything in human experience, as applied to methods of taxation, is settled, it certainly is the fact that taxation upon personal property never can be made a success. Taxes can be raised from personal property, no doubt; for large sums are thus raised; but that they cannot be levied with any reasonable approach to accuracy or equality is demonstrated, not only by conclusive reasoning, but by the more conclusive fact that they never have been thus levied. It is not for want of earnest and long sustained effort that the failure of this system of taxation has come to pass. For centuries the effort has been made; and for at least six centuries it was backed by all the power of a government which commanded the whole civilized world and which armed its tax-gatherers, not with the paltry weapons of oaths and penalties, but with the more substantial powers of indiscriminate search, the lash, the rack, the thumbscrew, the gridiron, and the cross. The Roman empire fell to pieces under the pressure of this vain effort to reach personal property by taxation.[1] The same thing was attempted, at a later period, in dealing with the Jews. It failed with them. They could be robbed and murdered; but they could not be regularly taxed.

That which all the tremendous power of Rome, in its grandest days, failed to accomplish, that which the infernal tortures of Spain could not accomplish, when it beheaded hundreds, burned thousands, and massacred tens of thousands, letting loose a brutal soldiery in a vain struggle to tax the Netherlands, American farmers are still apparently convinced that they can accomplish, by distributing blank forms, administering long oaths, and threatening penalties of fifty per cent. How far they have succeeded, governors, assessors, and tax commissions in New York, Ohio, Maryland, West Virginia, and many other States, have set forth again and again, lamenting the utter

[1] Gibbon mentions, quite as a matter of course, that fathers murdered their children, on a large scale, principally as a result of fear of tax-gatherers; that racks and scourges were freely used; that the approach of the tax-gatherer "was announced by the tears and terrors of the citizens"; and that false returns were punished with horrid deaths, as being both "treason and sacrilege" (*History*, ch. xiv. and xvii.). Savigny shows that the decurions, who governed the cities and were held responsible for the taxes, often sold themselves into slavery to escape the dreadful burden, but were dragged back to scourge their fellow-subjects (Smith's note, 2 Gibbon, 335, ed. 1862; 1 Savigny, *Hist. Roman Law*, 40: 2d ed,). Even a Massachusetts farmer could ask no greater efficiency than this.

failure of the system. Their complaints have become monotonous in their uniformity. Nothing, indeed, has been added to the sum of knowledge on this point, since the calm and detailed report of David A. Wells to the New York legislature, in 1871 ; in which the experience of that State and many other States was luminously set forth ; and it was made clear that taxes on personal property were nowhere equally assessed or efficiently collected.

§ 3. **Taxation by oath.** The result of the widespread maintenance of these taxes is to fill the land with liars and perjurers. In some States the business of perjury is mostly confined to the assessors ; who regularly make returns which they know to be false, but cannot make true.[1] In others, such as Ohio, Vermont, Connecticut, all the Southern States and most of the Western States, perjury is the business of the taxpayers.[2] Their scrupulous consciences, in many cases, find a way of escape by omitting, in fact, to take the oath which they sign ; and they are innocent of everything except lying. The delicately conscientious get some one to sign for them ; and where an oath is absolutely required, a considerate notary certifies to the oath before it is taken ; after which, of course, it is not taken at all. On surveying the whole field, however, one's faith in American truthfulness is cheered, and we entertain larger hopes for the future of humanity. For it appears that, where blanks are diligently circulated and oaths insisted upon, the average man will return ten, if not fifteen per cent. of his personal property ; whereas, in the absence of this appeal to piety, he will return nothing at all. This touching proof of American reverence for the sacred-

---

[1] Hon. Martin I. Townsend, Const. Conv., 1867 ; Auditor's Rep., Nebraska, 1894.

[2] Report Ohio Com., 1893 ; Ely on *Taxation ;* D. A. Wells's *Rept. on Local Taxation,* 1871.

ness of an oath reminds one of the famous Yankee who, hearing his father accused of having falsely warranted the quality of a trifle sold for " ninepence " (the New England eighth of a dollar) replied: " No ; the old man would never tell a lie for ninepence ; though he would tell eight of 'em for a dollar."

§ 4. **The Experience of New York.** How is it in the State of New York? One of the most experienced assessors in that State, Mr. George H. Andrews, addressing a legislative committee on October 6, 1874, said :

" No man and no corporation, banks only excepted, needs pay a tax upon personal property. Widows and orphants must pay. Upon them in the extremity of their distress, the law lays its heavy hand. It bereaves the bereaved. Moribund itself, it has an affinity for the effects of the dead. The records of the surrogate furnish the schedule, and the machinery of the law used in adjusting an estate is not sufficiently flexible to regularly permit such a transfer of securities as would insure an exemption."

As might well be expected, the State assessors, on January 21, 1874, reported " that less than fifteen per cent. of the personal property of the State liable to taxation finds a place on the rolls of the assessor, and that of mortgages, not over five per cent. of the value is assessed." In one town the proceeds of a single auction sale of cattle, belonging to one resident, amounted to $360,000; while the whole assessment of personal property in that town was $28,850 ; " a sum very much less than that obtained for one cow." The assessors say : " A large percentage of all the personal property assessed is found entered on the rolls to women, minor heirs, lunatics, who cannot watch with the eagle eye of business men, or to trustees or guardians." In some towns these classes held more than one half of all the personal property on the assessment roll. Two women, residing in the village of Batavia, were assessed for more personal property than all the individuals in the neighboring city of Rochester, with a population of 70,000. In one town a girl, mentioned in the assessment as a lunatic, was assessed $5000 for personal property; which the assessor stated was the full amount of her personal estate. All over the State "the amount of assessment depends more on the will, craft, conscience (or want of conscience) of the party assessed than upon the law or its enforcement."

The state of affairs has grown worse with each succeeding year. In 1892 a ridiculous law was passed, much lauded by the governor, requiring applicants for reduction of assessment to make oath that they had not incurred debts in the purchase of non-taxable property or for the purpose of avoiding taxation. It ought to have been entitled: "An act to punish truthfulness and to reward perjury."[1]

Experienced assessors in every state say that the most honest returns of property are always made by the poorer classes, and the most inadequate returns by millionaires; while widows, who have no experience in business, and trustees, who represent widows and orphans, are taxed upon every dollar that they own.

§ 5. **Experience of California.** The experience of California furnishes perhaps the latest example of the utter failure of all schemes for taxing personal property to work out anything like an approximation to justice.

In 1879 a new constitution was adopted. It was carried through solely by the farmers' votes; merchants, bankers, and capitalists, whether large or small, voting almost unanimously against it. Under this constitu-

---

[1] Who can tell just what is meant by "non-taxable property"? Hardly any two lawyers would at once agree upon a definition. And who can tell precisely for what "purpose" he incurred a debt? The statute is only one more premium upon either shrewdness or perjury.

tion and these laws, not only were bonds, money, and credits made taxable, without any deduction on account of debts, except from credits, and then only such debts as are due to residents of the State of California; but holders of stock in corporations were avowedly and intentionally subjected to double taxation, first, upon the corporate property, and again upon the capital stock, which is merely their evidence of title to that property. It was supposed, alike by the friends and enemies of the new constitution, that under its operation personal property of every description would be thoroughly reached, and at any rate, that whatever was by any chance overlooked would be more than made up by double taxation upon that which was found. The actual result has been to falsify all the predictions of both the friends and enemies of the constitution; for it has done almost none of the good or evil which was anticipated; for the reason that the capacity of the patriotic taxpayer to commit perjury, and the susceptibility of assessors to bribery had been altogether underestimated. Some of the results are positively ludicrous.

§ 6. **Poor California!** If the assessment returns are to be believed, in nine tenths of California there is not a pound of butter; in four fifths of the State the sheep do not produce any wool; fifty counties have quantities of beehives, but only four have any honey; personal property is vanishing from San Francisco; loans of money are becoming unknown in the rest of the State; municipal bonds of all kinds are not held within the State to an amount equal to one tenth of those outstanding; and, finally, money has been smitten by a pestilence, two thirds of all that was there before the adoption of the constitution having already taken to itself wings, and showing no sign of returning. One of the great objects of the new constitution was to tax railroad, telegraph, and telephone companies to the last cent of their value. The actual result has been that telegraph and telephone companies were assessed in 1886 for less than the cost of their bare poles, or about $65 per mile. The railroad companies resisted taxation for one or two years; at the end of which, by a singularly simultaneous impulse of virtue, some thirty boards of supervisors directed their district attorneys rigorously to prosecute the railroad companies to the uttermost of the law. Thirty district attorneys forthwith dragged the railroad companies before the judicial tribunals. With equal promptness the thirty boards of supervisors met, and, without any consultation with each other, passed resolutions directing the district attorneys to compromise all suits at 60 per cent. of the amount claimed; and the thirty district attorneys obeyed before the State officers could protest, even by telegraph.

The general result has been that the proportion of personal property to the whole assessed value of property has steadily fallen from 50 per cent. in 1861 to 34 per cent. in 1874, 26 per cent. in 1880, and $13\frac{1}{2}$ per cent. in 1894.

§ 7. **Cities relieved; farmers burdened.** The following table will show the working of a series of measures which were expected, above all things, to increase the burdens of taxation upon San Francisco on personal property, and especially upon money. For convenience, thousands are omitted in this table, and the figures "000" must be added in every case:

CALIFORNIA ASSESSMENTS
IN THOUSANDS OF DOLLARS.

1880.	Land.	Improvements on Land.	Money.	Other Personal Property.	Total.
San Francisco	122,030	42,969	19,747	68,584	253,330
Remainder of State.	227,127	68,568	4,931	81,072	381,698
	349,157	111,537	24,678	149,656	635,028
1886.					
San Francisco	120,375	55,034	6,188	48,705	230,302
Remainder of State.	340,274	100,775	2,887	94,022	537,953
	460,649	155,809	9,075	142,727	768,255
1894.					
San Francisco	178,000	83,879	7,100	56,130	325,109
Remainder of State.	537,000	160,935	3,187	89,430	791,043
	715,000	244,814	10,287	145,560	1,116,152

In the foregoing table no account is taken of railroads which are separately assessed by State officers. There was an increase in the valuation of railroads from $31,174,000 in 1880 to $48,051,000 in 1886, which was reduced in 1894 to $42,730,640; of course nearly all outside of San Francisco. The valuation of San Francisco in 1894 was arbitrarily increased by the State officers 15 per cent. above the figures here given.

In reviewing this table it will be seen that while improvements upon land in San Francisco increased about one third in six years, money fell off more than two thirds, and other personal property nearly one third. In the rest of the State, which is mainly agricultural, the value of improvements increased nearly one half; personal property, other than money, increased nearly one sixth; while the loss of money among the farmers, though severe, did not compare with the affliction which befell the capitalists of San Francisco. The general result was to reduce the share of San Francisco in the State tax from 40 per cent. to 30 per cent. In other words, the city paid 25 per cent. *less,* and the farmers 16⅔ per cent. *more.*

This result has continued ever since. The assessments for 1894 show that San Francisco still pays only 31 per cent. of the State taxes on property outside of railroads. And even this result is only obtained by an arbitrary increase of 15 per cent. in the city's share by State officers.

§ 8. **Taxation of merchandise and bonds.** Looking into the details of personal property, attention is naturally attracted toward the three items of merchandise, bonds, and credits; all of which it was supposed that the new methods of assessment would reach to a degree never before known.

The actual result was as follows :

CALIFORNIA ASSESSMENTS

IN THOUSANDS OF DOLLARS.

	Mdse.	Bonds.	Credits.	Total.
1880.				
San Francisco	16,146	2,311	5,973	24,430
Remainder of State	11,504	729	14,740	26,973
	27,650	3,040	20,713	51,403
1886.				
San Francisco	15,713	449	6,379	22,541
Remainder of State	15,042	678	6,211	21,931
	30,755	1,127	12,590	44,472
1894.				
San Francisco	16,123	3,696	8,474	28,293
Remainder of State	17,462	128	5,858	23,448
	33,585	3,824	14,332	51,741

Here it appears that a very small increase (less than one per cent.) has been returned at the end of fourteen years; all of which dates only from 1892, up to which time the return bonds continued insignificant.

§ 9. **Experience of Boston.** According to unanimous testimony, the city of Boston is so fortunate as to possess a board of assessors, in whose honesty and ability every one has confidence, and who are fanatical believers in the taxation of personal property. These assessors are armed by law with almost despotic powers of search and with absolutely despotic powers of valuation. They can ransack every man's books; they can disregard all the evidence, when they have finished. After exhausting all their powers of inquiry, they are allowed to meet in secret, to go through a process of arbitrary assessment, fitly known by the name of "dooming." Their return of details for the year 1889 showed that the whole amount of taxable property, which they were actually able to discover, was $39,000,000, exclusive of bank stock. Being dissatisfied with this estimate, which was all that was justified by any facts which they could state, they proceeded to multiply it four and a half times by a mere guess. In their dooming chamber they guessed that personal property, other than bank stock, ought to be valued at $186,000,000; and the citizens of Boston were compelled to pay taxes upon that amount. Could anything be more monstrous or more absurd than a system of taxation which, even when administered by phenomenally honest and competent men, produces such results?

The items of which the $39,000,000 actually discovered consist are in the following proportions, in round numbers:

Visible to assessors.................. ....$14,570,000 or $37\frac{3}{8}\%$
Invisible to them........................24,650,000 or $62\frac{5}{8}\%$

Almost the whole of the things visible to Boston assessors consisted of merchandise and machinery. Taxes upon these, of course, if equally distributed, simply increased the cost of goods to consumers, just as excise duties on whisky increase the cost of whisky to drinkers. But it is manifest, from the arbitrary increase made by the assessors, that these taxes were *not* equally distributed and therefore one large section of taxpayers was robbed for the benefit of the other section. For unequal taxation upon producers makes it impossible for those who are taxed beyond their just share to recover such excess from their customers; while those who are taxed below their share recover all which they would have paid under strictly equal taxation. It follows that those who are taxed most are simply plundered, under forms of law, for the profit of their competitors who are taxed least. If Havemeyer and Spreckels were the only refiners of sugar, and both were taxed equally upon their production, both would recover the tax from their customers. But if Havemeyer should be taxed, while Spreckels went free, Spreckels could undersell Havemeyer, who would be practically robbed for Spreckels' benefit.

§ 10. **Double taxation.** Passing to the invisible property assessed in Boston, we find that $4,000,000 consisted of cash, $7,700,000 of stock in foreign corporations, and $12,500,000 of debts, of which two thirds were secured by mortgage on real estate. Thus more than half of all the personal property returned for taxation consisted of mere paper titles to or liens against other things, which were taxed somewhere else. If this is not double taxation, what is?

See how the system works. Smith forms a little corporation, to own a railroad in Vermont. The railroad is fully taxed there. But Smith lives in Boston; and, as he owns all the stock, say $100,000, and stock in a foreign corporation is assessed there, he is taxed on the whole amount a second time. He mortgages the road for $100,000, and spends the proceeds on improvements. This additional value is taxed in Vermont. But he sells the mortgage bonds to Brown, of Boston; who is thus taxed again upon the whole $100,000 there. Brown pledges the bonds to Jones, as security for a loan of $100,000; and forthwith Jones is taxed upon the whole amount. This makes three taxes upon only one piece of real property.

This is the way in which the wise men of Massachusetts mean that their laws shall work; but as the taxpayers revolt against such injustice, and protect themselves in the only way open to them, to wit, by hard swearing or by refusing to make returns, Massachusetts counteracts that evil, by imposing an arbitrary tax upon those who do not make returns, four times as large as is paid by those who do.

In Illinois an even more drastic method prevails. A Board of Equalization, if of opinion that the valuation of any county is too low, increases everybody's taxes fourfold, on the assumption that all have made false returns alike. Thus the conscientious taxpayer is made to feel that virtue must indeed be its own reward.

CHAPTER VI.

Effect of the Personalty Tax on Farmers.

§ 1. The question stated. Of course there are some forms of personal property which can be seen and appraised by the assessors, almost as readily as real estate, though not with so correct an estimate of value. The objection to taxation of chattels is not that none of them can be taxed; it is that so many of them can be and are reached, while so many more are not, that the tax is necessarily unequal and unjust. The important question, therefore, is, upon what class does this tax bear most oppressively? Is that class the more wealthy or the less wealthy? Is it the city population or the farmers? If taxes were levied only upon the value of real estate, would the farmers pay more or less of the whole taxes than they do now?

Farmers in general have been long convinced that the rigid taxation of personal property would relieve their burdens; and it is entirely by their votes that the existing system is maintained. This is all theory on their part. They have not studied the facts and know nothing about them. They assume that "it must be so."

But let us study the facts, before discussing any theory.

Any attempt to separate the community into two distinct classes, one of which is taxable only on real estate and the other of which is taxable only on personal property, is obviously impossible and absurd. No man is ever reached by the tax-gatherer, who does not occupy some piece of land. If he did not, the tax-collector would never find him. Tramps pay no direct taxes. Neither can any man live without occupying some improvements on real estate and possessing some personal property. Every taxpayer, without exception, is an occupant of land and improvements upon land, and an owner of personal property. The only selfish interest which any taxpayer has, in deciding between rival systems of taxation, is to know which will produce a sufficient revenue to the state, with the smallest possible burden to him. In considering, therefore, the interest of any class, such as farmers, the real question to be answered is not whether they in fact own more or less personal property than merchants, bankers, and money lenders. The questions to be answered are:

1. Do farmers own less personal property, *in proportion to the value of their land*, than do those other classes?

2. Are the particular kinds of personal property which they own less easily reached by the tax-gatherer, than are the kinds of property owned by the other classes?

The state must raise a certain fixed amount for public purposes. This amount it will assess upon all taxpayers, in proportion to the value of their property, as reported by the assessors; not in proportion to its *real* value; which the assessors, of course, are never able exactly to ascertain. If, therefore, experience proves that assessors are able to find *twenty* times as much land value in the possession of merchants as they can among farmers, but only *ten* times as much personal property among merchants as they find among farmers, it is a plain result, as simple as the rule of three, that *the taxation of personal property will end in making farmers pay a larger proportion of the taxes* than they would pay if all taxes were concentrated on the value of real estate.

§ 2. **The farmer's idea.** Now the average farmer, no doubt, says at once that this is impossible. He owns, we will say, 100 acres of land ; and he knows of no merchant in any of the great cities who owns as much as one acre. He owns neither stock nor bonds, and has only $500 in the bank. He knows of 1000 merchants or money lenders who each own $100,000 or $1,000,000 in stocks and bonds and keep balances of $50,000 in the bank. To him, therefore, it seems plain that the exemption of personal property from taxation must make him pay much more, in proportion to his means, than the merchant and banker.

§ 3. **The farmer's error.** But the farmer, in reasoning thus, entirely overlooks the most important facts of the problem, and abandons the common-sense of which he so much boasts. That common-sense would tell him that, just as his one hundred acres are worth far more than 100,000 acres in the midst of Africa, so one tenth of an acre in the heart of a large city is worth more than all his farm. It would also tell him that the assessor can easily count his cattle, horses, sheep, and hogs, and estimate pretty correctly the value of his house and barns ; whereas, the most expert assessor can never find out how many bonds the banker owns, unless he can persuade that banker to tell him ; while in estimating the value of the banker's house and furniture, he might guess at $10,000, $25,000, or $50,000, with a perfectly equal chance of being right or wrong in either case. The banker has chairs standing side by side, apparently of exactly equal value, but one of which cost $25 and the other $250. He has two paintings, one of which is five times as large as the other, and which the honest farmer would, therefore, think to be five times as valuable ; whereas in fact the large picture is barely worth $500, while the small one would sell as quick as lightning for $20,000. There are many houses, in large cities, upon the interior decoration of which the owners have spent more than $100,000. The most experienced assessors would fail to discover that these decorations were really more costly than those in adjoining houses, which in fact did not cost one tenth of that amount.

§ 4. **Taxation of franchises.** Nor is the difficulty of this problem confined to the difficulty which the assessor finds in doing his work. Vast amounts of what are commonly called personal property, and, indeed, the bulk of those things which the average farmer seeks to tax as personal property, consist of really nothing but rights over real estate. Thus the value of bonds of a railroad corporation consists very largely in the land which the company covers by its tracks, engine house, stations, etc.; and the stock of such corporations represents practically nothing else. The franchises of such corporations, which, of course, constitute a larger part of the value of both stocks and bonds, really consist of nothing but the right to use certain tracts of land, to the exclusion of all other persons. Under any proper assessment of the value of land, those franchises would be assessed at their full value; because the franchise of exclusive use is all that gives to any land its commercial value. A system of taxation upon the full value of land would, therefore, levy taxes upon every dollar which corporate franchises are worth. No system of taxation on personal property is needed in the smallest degree for this purpose. It is indeed only a hindrance to it and a convenient means of evading taxation; for the assessor, not being allowed to compute this value, in estimating the value of the land, has to take his chances of finding it under the name of personal property. All mortgages on land are, of course, practically interests in the land itself, and would be fully taxed under a system of taxation confined to the value of the land. The tax may be collected from either the mortgagor or the mortgagee, as the legislature should think fit. Either plan is perfectly consistent with the exemption of personal property from taxation.

§ 5. **The experience of Ohio.** In the light of these considerations, let us review some of the statistics furnished from year to year by the official reports of assessors in Ohio, as compiled annually in the auditor's report. For the purpose of such comparison let us set on one side the four counties which include all the largest cities, and on the other side the five counties which contain the smallest proportion of city population among all the counties of Ohio.

The former, which we will call the city counties, include Hamilton, Cuyahoga, Franklin, and Lucas, with the cities of Cincinnati, Cleveland, Columbus, and Toledo.

The latter, which we will call the rural counties, are Geauga, Noble, Carroll, Medina, and Monroe.

These counties respectively represent the extreme contrasts between the cities and the farms of the State. Thus, in Hamilton and Cuyahoga, the assessed value of town lots is about seven times the assessed value of the farms; whereas, in the five rural counties, the assessed value of farms is nowhere less than ten times that of town lots, while, in Geauga County, the farm lots are worth twenty-seven times as much as the town lots. Hamilton County, which includes Cincinnati, is the typical city county of Ohio; while Geauga, which includes no large town, is the typical rural county.

§ 6. **Farmers pay largest share of taxes on personal property.** Now, the first thing which strikes the eye, on

EFFECT OF THE PERSONALTY TAX ON FARMERS. 89

looking over the statistics of these counties, is the following comparison:

Ohio Valuations, 1887.

	Assessed Val. of Real Est.	Assessed Val. of Chattels.
City counties	$317,854,665	$113,340,087
Rural counties	29,733,450	14,307,668

Any one can see that, in the counties which include all the large cities, the assessed value of personal property is only about one fourth of the whole assessment; while in the rural counties, personal property constitutes very nearly one third of their whole assessed value. In more exact figures, the value of assessed personal property in the city counties is $26\frac{1}{4}$ per cent. of the whole, while in the rural counties it is $32\frac{1}{2}$ per cent. If, therefore, all personal property should be exempted from taxation, the farmers of these five exclusively rural counties would pay 8 per cent. *less* taxes than they do now.

That this result is not a mere accident, owing to some peculiar condition of these particular counties, is easily proved by testing the same question in other ways. Thus, if we set apart the four great city counties and compare them with all the rest of the State, including farming districts and smaller towns indiscriminately, we find substantially the same result, as follows:

Ohio Valuations, 1887.

	Real Estate.	Personal Property.
City counties	$317,854,665	$113,340,087
Remainder of State	867,155,960	406,832,007

Here, in the counties which include all the great cities, personal property amounts to $26\frac{1}{4}$ per cent. of the whole valuation; while in the remainder of the State it amounts to 32 per cent.

But if we compare single counties, such as Hamilton, in which town lots compose about 85 per cent. of all the real estate, with Medina, in which town lots compose only 10 per cent. of the real estate, we find the result as follows:

Ohio Valuations, 1887.

	Real Estate.	Personal Property.
Hamilton	$163,732,580	$53,144,182
Medina	8,304,740	5,012,304

Here we find that the real estate of Hamilton Gounty is assessed at *twenty* times the value of Medina County; while the personal property of Hamilton is assessed at less than *eleven* times that of Medina. Personal property constitutes $24\frac{1}{2}$ per cent. of the valuation of Hamilton, and $37\frac{1}{2}$ per cent. of the valuation of Medina. The total exemption of personal property from taxation, therefore, would, if taxes were divided only between the counties of Hamilton and Medina, relieve the farmers of Medina from exactly *one sixth* of their present burdens. Invariably, farmers are compelled to pay a much larger share of State taxation, as the result of taxing personal property.

§ 8. **Taxation of credits heaviest on farmers.** But let us test this question in still other ways. The chief clamor in favor of taxing personal property has been directed toward the taxation of moneys and credits. The money lender, who is supposed to have vast sums on deposit in bank, and the merchant, who is supposed to have vast outstanding credits due from the poor farmers, are the special objects against whom this method of taxation is aimed—all for the relief of the farmers. Let us see how this works, by a comparison of the same typical counties. The Ohio report for 1887 shows that their relative assessments were as follows:

1887.	Real Estate.	Money.	Credits, etc.
City counties........	$317,854,665	$5,328,050	$13,291,833
Rural counties.......	29,733,450	907,829	4,384,381

Roughly stated, it thus appears that if taxation were confined to real estate alone, the city counties would pay *eleven* times as much as the rural counties; whereas, if taxation were levied on money alone, they would pay less than *six* times as much, and if levied on credits alone, a little more than *three* times as much; while, if taxation were levied on both money and credits, they would pay about *four* times as much. Consequently, the burden of taxation in rural counties as compared with the large cities is nearly three times as heavy on money and credits as it is on real estate. *The only result, therefore, of taxing money, credits, and similar investments, is to relieve the burden of the cities and increase the burden of the farms.*

Let us test this particular illustration by comparing the County of Hamilton, in which town lots are worth seven times as much as farm lands, with Geauga, in which farm lands are worth twenty-seven times as much as town lots:

1887.	Real Estate.	Money.	Credits.
Hamilton	$162,732,580	$1,833,279	$,735,945
Geauga..............	5,555,800	282,118	534,477

Roughly stated, Hamilton County is assessed for nearly thirty times as much real estate, less than seven times as much money, and less than eleven times as much credits as Geauga County. If taxation were levied exclusively upon money on hand, Geauga County would pay between four and five times as much as it would if the taxes were levied exclusively on real estate. If taxes were levied solely upon credits, Geauga would pay nearly three times as much as it would if they were levied solely on real estate. There is not much evidence here of any advantage gained by the farmer, through his diligent search after the money lender and the creditor.

§ 9. The more effective the system, the worse for the farmers. For many years, and in fact persistently ever since 1846, when Ohio adopted the present system of taxation, Ohio farmers have been clamoring more and more loudly for protection from unjust taxation, for greater burdens upon merchants and bankers, and for more stringent enforcement of the law. The tax and assessment laws have been amended, again and again, in obedience to this demand ; and State officers have been continually more persistent in their efforts to shift the burden of taxation from farmers to capitalists, by means of a rigorous enforcement of taxation upon personal property. A spy law has been enacted, giving 20 per cent. or more to any spy who will expose false returns of personalty. Let us, therefore, inquire whether there is any tendency to improvement in these respects, and whether the history of the last few years encourages the hope that the evasions of the "Shylocks" can be put an end to and the honest farmer relieved by a more thorough assessment of personal property. For this purpose let us again compare the typical counties of Hamilton and Geauga—the former having an almost exclusively city population and the latter being occupied almost exclusively by farmers, having no village with more than 1000 inhabitants.

§ 10. Watches, carriages, and money. If there are any items in which the Shylocks ought to make a better showing than the farmers, surely watches, pleasure carriages, money on hand, and credits would stand first on the list. Let us take them in succession :

Number of Watches.	1882.	1887.
Ohio	118,286	114,631
Hamilton	9,283	8,659
Geauga	845	922

These statistics tell a sorrowful tale of poverty and destitution among the poor farmers of Cincinnati; while they indicate that the bloated capitalists of Geauga County are the chief patrons of the fine watchmakers of Paris and Geneva. Let us turn from this sorrowful picture to

Pleasure Carriages.	1882.	1887.
Ohio	254,918	224,440
Hamilton	13,710	9,854
Geauga	2,488	1,717

Here one finds some slight relief, not, indeed, in the increasing prosperity of any part of Ohio, but in the fact that the poor farmers of Cincinnati do not seem to have given up any larger proportion of their pleasure carriages than the Shylocks of Geauga ; while a desolating wave of poverty has swept over the entire State, resulting in the loss of nearly one eighth of all its vehicles. Walking is evidently becoming fashionable in Ohio. Let us look at

Money on Hand.	1882.	1887.
Ohio	$46,160,629	$35,132,131
Hamilton	2,321,502	1,833,279
Geauga	352,053	282,118

Here, again, a wave of poverty has flooded the whole State, in tolerably equal proportions. Money is evidently rapidly vanishing ; for the total stock of the State has fallen off $11,000,000 in five years, diminishing 25 per cent. in Hamilton, but only 20 per cent. in Geauga. We will now look at

Credits.	1882.	1887.
Ohio	$104,838,938	$106,173,894
Hamilton	6,571,829	5,735,945
Geauga	560,693	534,477

Here we see that Ohio, as a state, is a money lender to the extent of one per cent. more in 1887 than in 1882. But again the poor agriculturists of Cincinnati come to the front, with a loss of $836,000, or 12½ per cent. of their total stock; while the loss in Geauga County is only about one third as much, or a trifle over 4 per cent.

§ 11. **How Ohio watches go.** In reviewing this sad picture of decline, one is reminded of Goldsmith's melancholy words:

> "Where wealth accumulates and men decay."

But in Ohio it appears that men accumulate and wealth decays; for the population of the State has largely increased, while its wealth is apparently ebbing away. Truly was it said by the wise man of old, that "riches have wings"; for the disappearance of money from Ohio conclusively proves it. Looking at the returns of carriages, one is tempted to think that the principal reason why they have wheels is to enable the owners to take them out of Ohio; and as for the watches, they are certainly not open to the accusation so often brought against French clocks, that they will "never go." Ohio watches certainly can and do "go," with a rapidity and steadiness not often equalled.[1]

§ 12. **Ohio in 1892.** The foregoing statistics were prepared in 1889; and as no substantial change has taken place in the methods or success of Ohio taxation, it has not seemed worth while to go to the trouble of correcting these statistics by the latest information. But to prove that these figures are just as applicable now as they were in 1887, a few statistics will be given from the official reports of 1892.

---

[1] The speed of Cincinnati watches has lately increased. The latest report shows that 20 per cent. have "gone," in the last six years, against only 8 per cent. in the previous six years. The speed of Ohio carriages is even greater; 25 per cent. having gone in six years. The honest farmers have taken the hint, and have dropped 58,000 carriages out of sight—of the assessors. Perhaps the owners have taken to bicycles instead.

By authority of the Legislature of Ohio, Hon. Wm. McKinley, Governor of that State, appointed a tax commission of four members; two being Republicans and two Democrats, but all professing themselves in favor of continuing the tax on personal property. Their report, presented to the Governor on December 23, 1893, confirms all which has been said above. It shows, moreover, that the disproportion between burdens imposed by the tax on personal property upon the cities and upon the farming districts, respectively, has increased considerably since 1887. A few comparisons are here given between the assessments in 1887 and 1892 in Hamilton and Geauga Counties respectively.

Money on Hand.

County.	1882.	1887.	1892.
Hamilton....	$2,321,502	$1,833,279	$1,535,375
Geauga......	352,053	282,118	451,567

Here it will be seen that the amount of taxable money reported in Geauga, which is a purely farming district, has largely increased, owing to the spy system established by the State. But the amount of taxable money reported in Hamilton County, which includes the great city of Cincinnati, has again largely decreased; the spy system having entirely failed there.

We will now compare results in

Credits.

County.	1882.	1887.	1892.
Hamilton....	$6,571,029	$5,735,945	$4,289,901
Geauga......	560,693	534,477	507,651

Although there has been a shrinkage of about 5 per cent. in the taxable credits of Geauga, since 1887, that is nothing, compared with the 28 per cent. reduction in Cincinnati.

The Tax Commission Report gives many other most

instructive figures; too many to be repeated here. To mention, however, a few examples, it appears that the County of Lucas, which contains "the flourishing city of Toledo," is rapidly increasing in population, and has more than double the stationary population of Muskingum County, nevertheless returned in 1892 very much less than half as much intangible personal property for taxation, little more than one third as much in credits, and not nearly one third as much in money. Thus the rural county is taxed thrice as heavily as the city. The County of Cuyahoga, including the great city of Cleveland, the population of which is rapidly increasing, and is already about twenty-five times as large as that of Geauga County, returned for taxation less than four times as much money, and much less than seven times as much credits. Thus Geauga was taxed, upon these values, about five times as heavily as Cuyahoga.

The net result of all the comparisons made by the commissioners, between city and farming districts, is to prove that *the tax upon personal property makes farmers pay from $4 to $7, where it makes city residents pay $1.*

The preposterous nature of returns of personal property for taxation is further illustrated in the report of the Commission, by comparison of the amounts of money on hand or on deposit, thus returned, with the amounts actually held on deposit in banks, within the cities making these returns. The following examples will show the general drift.

Deposits (Partly Estimated).

1892.	Deposits in Bank.	Deposits Taxed.
Cincinnati	$29,000,000	$1,300,000
Cleveland	63,000,000	1,000,000
Toledo	8,120,000	253,000

Here again the farmers come to the front, to bear their share of taxation with a generous hand ; for while five counties, containing all the large cities, held on deposit in banks $120,000,000, and returned for taxation only $6,000,000, the remainder of the State, including all the farming districts, having only $70,000,000 in banks, returned for taxation over $32,000,000. That is, having 40 per cent. *less*, they were taxed 450 per cent. *more !* *So the tax on " money " bears upon farmers about ten times as heavily as upon city residents.*

§ 13. **Conclusions of the Commission.** No wonder that the Commission, after giving many more illustrations, concluded by saying : " It is useless to pursue this subject further . . . While in the country counties . . . taxation of intangible property is perhaps feasible, it is in city counties an utter failure. . . . It is confidently believed that no appreciable part of the intangible property existing in the city counties is reached by our method of taxation. *It is the country counties which pay the taxes upon personal property.*"

The Commissioners further say : " It is to be remembered that we have in this State an extremely rigid system." They show that personal property is pursued with more severity and ingenuity in Ohio than in any other State ; and notwithstanding all this, they declare that the system is " an utter failure," and that even with the respect to the spy law of Ohio, " this scheme, like all other attempts to reach intangible property, follows the universal law . . . that the large cities escape, and the country counties feel its burden." Again they say : " The system as it is actually administered results in debauching the moral sense. It is a school of perjury. It sends large amounts of property into hiding. It drives capital in large quantities from the State. . . . The moral sense of the community is blunted ; its citizens are made familiar with all manner of evasion ; they are taught to lie."

§ 14. **Experience of Missouri.** Lest it should be imagined that the experience of Ohio is peculiar, let us inquire into the experience of Missouri, which is even more decidedly than Ohio an agricultural State. In Missouri there are only four cities of over 15,000 population, and only three of over 25,000. Only four counties show a decided preponderance of town-lot values over farm values; and only two more even the smallest difference that way, and those for one year only.

The four counties in which all cities worthy of the name are situated, are Buchanan, Greene, Jackson, and St. Louis City. These we will call the city counties and the others the rural counties. The following are the official and latest published

Missouri Valuations, 1893 (in Thousands of Dollars).

	Farm Lands.	Town Lots.	Total Real Estate.	Personal Property.
4 city counties....	29,572	320,177	349,749	70,161
101 rural counties.	277,348	67,524	344,872	159,514
Total........	306,920	387,701	694,621	229,675

Here it can be seen at a glance that the four cities, with their adjoining counties, in which farms form much less than one tenth of the whole value of real estate, pay taxes on *more than one half of all the real estate* in Missouri, but on much *less than one third of its personal property*. Personal property in the cities amounts to less than 20 per cent. of their real estate; while in the rural counties it amounts to 46 per cent. of real estate. The farmers of Missouri pay 1½ per cent. *less* taxes on their land than the cities pay, but 127 per cent. *more* on personal property. Even in the eight poorest counties in Missouri, where farm lands are worth from twenty to one hundred times as much as town lots, personal property is assessed at 40 per cent. of real estate; so that the poorest farmers of the State pay 100 per cent. more taxes on personal property than do the richest cities, in proportion to their real estate.

Let us compare St. Louis City with the rest of the State:

Missouri Assessments, 1893.

	Real Estate.	Personalty.	Money, Notes, etc.
St. Louis	$259,781,100	$44,341,110	$8,449,790
Rest of State	434,839,557	185,334,285	67,663,576
Total	$694,620,657	$229,675,395	$76,113,366

These figures show that, while St. Louis pays about 40 per cent. of the taxes on real estate, it pays less than 20 per cent. of the taxes on all personal property, and just 11 per cent. of the taxes on money and credits. The rest of the State pays 70 per cent. more on land than St. Louis does, but 318 per cent. more on personal property in general, and exactly 700 per cent. more on money and credits! Yet Missouri is governed entirely by the farm vote, and it "enjoys" a general property tax as severe and all-reaching as the farmers are able to invent. The only result of their ingenuity is, as usual, to load heavier burdens upon their own shoulders.

§ 15. **The moon-struck theorists.** Figures like these might be collected, not only from Ohio and Missouri, but from every State and country under the sun, where statistics are kept and personal property is taxed. *They* are the moon-struck theorists, who, in defiance of all the facts and all the experience of the world, persist in the vain endeavor to tax personal property and in the absurd assertion that this form of taxation tends to relieve farmers.

Farmers cannot conceal their sheep and oxen, their plows and implements; and they have enormous difficulty in concealing their wealth in any form, because their

affairs are so well known to all their neighbors. If they
have any money in bank, all the village knows it. If
they have loaned money or sold goods on credit, their
debtor is pretty sure to be some one in the immediate
neighborhood; and all the circumstances are known to
fifty people. The average farmer, when making his returns to the assessor, is afraid to understate his wealth
very greatly; because he could hardly look the assessor in
the face after doing so, being conscious that, if the assess-
or does not already know the truth, he can with very
little difficulty find it out for himself. But in large towns
and cities scarcely any man knows intimately the affairs
of his neighbor; and the assessor knows least of all. People are reputed to be worth $1,000,000, who in reality are
not worth $50,000; and others are reputed to be worth
only $100,000, who in reality are worth $2,000,000. Even
if the amount of any man's wealth is approximately
known, none of his neighbors know how that wealth is
invested, unless it is put in real estate. City assessors,
therefore, have absolutely no means of ascertaining the
value of any man's personal property, except by returns
from that man himself, or from the corporations with
whom he may happen to invest. If an Ohio man makes
his principal investments in corporations outside of the
State, the assessor is entirely at the mercy of the taxpayers. He can tell any number of lies with impunity.
The assessor rarely or never examines his books of account; and if assessors once began to make such an examination, many rich men would cease to keep books of
account at all, as it is notorious that they did when the
income tax was in existence between 1864 and 1872. All
things combine to make it easy for the assessor to reach
the farmer's personal property, and difficult for him to
reach that of the merchant, banker, or city capitalist.

CHAPTER VII.

TAXATION OF WOMEN AND CHILDREN.

§ 1. **Women and children fully taxed.** One of the worst features of the tax on personal property is that it always and everywhere bears with peculiar severity upon women and children. Their lot would be hard enough, even if they paid no more than their equal share, in proportion to their means; because none of them have the same power to replace the tax by fresh earnings, which men have, and most women and nearly all children, who are reached by this tax, have no such power at all. Most women thus taxed are widows, who have spent their lives in the family, and have no training for any occupation outside of the home. Their husbands or fathers have left them a little wealth, upon which to support themselves and their children. Even the most equally apportioned taxation inflicts upon them a loss for which they can have no remedy, such as a man has, in some new effort of industry.

But to that extent the burden, while it calls for sympathy, does not make any claim upon absolute justice. Far otherwise is it with the inequality of taxation which imposes upon women and children a burden rarely less than twice and frequently four or five times as heavy as that which it imposes upon active business men. It is this, and only this, to which attention is now invited.

§ 2. Taxation of women, through trustees. All personal property of children, most of the personal property of widows, and a large proportion of that held for other women, are held in the names of trustees. Probably nine tenths of these trust estates are created by the wills of deceased persons. All such trusts pass through courts of probate; the wills are recorded for public inspection; the courts always can and generally do require a full statement of the value of the property to be filed; accounts of its disposition are also filed; and all of these records are freely open to the assessors. It inevitably follows that such estates are assessed to their full value. Some friend of the testator is usually made executor and trustee. Will he take a false oath, simply to protect the widow and children of his best friend from taxation? Every consideration of patriotism, of manhood and piety gives him a chill of horror at the bare thought! Never, while an American heart beats true within his manly bosom, will he commit the smallest perjury, for the benefit of any one—except himself. Not even the most hardened professional oath-taker will degrade his honor by such treachery to his country and such defiance of his Maker. For how can he ask the widow to compensate him for such a service? And shall he put his immortal soul in peril for nought? No: the executor of any will, who is not also the principal legatee, may be trusted implicitly to make a true return.

Thus the personal property of most women and of all children is correctly reported in a place, where the assessors cannot help seeing the report. For one year, at least, it is taxed up to its full value.

Nor does the matter end there. The assessors, being once on the track, keep in pursuit. Unless some great change is made in the nature of the investments, the tax is never reduced. The property of all children and of most women is held permanently by trustees. Such trustees are confined strictly to a limited class of investments, most of which are taxable; while such as are not produce a very small income. Trustees have no power to evade taxation by running into debt. They are required to make oath to annual returns of the taxable property in their charge; and this duty they perform with the same pious conscientiousness which characterized their first returns. All property held in trust is therefore taxed for every dollar which it is worth, with few exceptions. Instances have been known where trustees have been base enough to evade taxation upon trust funds, for the sole benefit of those who are dependent upon their aid, without even the compensation of thanks from their innocent and unsuspecting beneficiaries. But, for the honor of human nature, let us hope that such gratuitous wickedness is rare.

§ 3. **Women's tax returns honest.** If a widow is herself sole executrix, she never thinks of taking a false oath, to evade taxation; and she has never learned the art of so arranging her investments as to avoid taxation. But if she had, she could not collect her thoughts sufficiently, in the first sense of her loss, to exercise her shrewdness immediately upon offering her husband's will for probate. Until the will is proved, she cannot touch the property; and therefore it must be and is filed speedily after her husband's death. At the same time, an affidavit of the value of the estate must be filed; and this is sharply scrutinized by officials, whose sole anxiety is to get taxes for the State, and who are certainly not open to small bribes, nor, generally speaking, to large ones. But if they were, the widow would not know how to reach them. Widows' returns, therefore, are always true.

In many cases widows and sisters receive bequests free

of trust. The result, however, is not materially different. They seek advice from the most honest man whom they know; and how can he look them in the face, while advising them to resort to the usual methods of evading taxation? Or, if he does, how can they carry out his advice? They are generally too simple-minded to want such advice or to act upon it, if given. Widows and their daughters can be seen in every tax office, asking advice, in their simplicity, from the tax collectors, as to what they ought to return for taxation. The writer has witnessed such scenes, and has heard the officials give advice, in fatherly tones, calling, not merely for a return of the last penny which the victims possessed, but also for returns of property which had been declared exempt by the highest judicial tribunal of the State. Noble public servants! They would extract the last drop of a widow's blood, for the profit of the government to which their loyalty is due!

§ 4. **Women taxed: men relieved.** Contrast the situation of these helpless women with that of the average man. His property is in his own hands. No probate court keeps any record of it; or, if it has come to him through the court, he speedily makes such changes, real or nominal, in the form of investments, as enable him truthfully to say that none of the original investments remain. In those States where deductions for debt are allowed, he can run into debt, to some complacent friend, to an amount sufficient to relieve him entirely from taxation. In other States, he can give away substantially all his taxable personable property on the day before assessment day, taking it back the next day. Or, if not shrewd enough or trustful enough to arrange his affairs in any of these ways, he can get rid of most of the tax by simply taking a false oath. That such oaths are taken in enormous numbers, wherever they are necessary to escape taxation, is proved by the universal testimony of assessors, in every part of the country. It is proved more conclusively, by reference to the tax returns of Ohio and California, elsewhere given.

The general result is that, while women and children are taxed upon nearly the full value of all taxable personal property in their possession, men are taxed upon less than one third of similar property belonging to them ; while the great majority of men pay taxes upon a far smaller proportion than that. The effect is to make women and children pay, at the very least, three times as large a share of such taxes as is paid by men.

It is difficult to speak with moderation of such methods and such results. Yet a recital of such iniquities is listened to by the very best Americans with perfect calmness, and by legislators with stolid indifference. The story of robbery, under the forms of law, in these cases, is usually dismissed with a cheap and vulgar sneer at "widows and orphans." The hearts of our people are hardened by the universal injustice, oppression, and iniquity of our methods of taxation. "None calleth for justice ; nor any pleadeth for truth."[1]

[1] Isaiah, lix., 4.

CHAPTER VIII.

Taxation of Improvements.

§ 1. Should improvements be taxed? Buildings and most other improvements upon land are easily visible, and they cannot easily be removed; and therefore it seems to most superficial thinkers that such improvements are certainly proper subjects for direct taxation.

But it is obvious that most of the reasons for the exemption of visible chattels from taxation apply with equal force to improvements upon land. These are really nothing but chattels attached to land; and the fact that they are so attached makes no difference in their real nature, and should not lead to their taxation.

A little consideration will make it clear that a tax upon improvements is not, in the long run, a strictly direct tax. If the building taxed is occupied by the owner as a residence the tax is levied upon and in proportion to his living expenses, just like a strictly revenue tariff. If he occupies it only for business purposes the tax must, in the long run, be added to his ordinary business profits; otherwise he would be driven out of business by the competition of others, who were able to recover such taxes from their customers. If he rents the building to others they must repay the tax; otherwise no one would put up new buildings to supply the demand of increasing population. Thus in any case taxes upon improvements are indirect taxes, which must be in the end repaid to the original taxpayer, with a profit out of the earnings of the masses. Like tariff taxes, they are eventually paid by men in proportion to what they spend, not what they have. They, therefore, bear with far more severity upon the poor than upon the rich; and they tend, like tariff taxes, to increase the inequality between the two classes.

Moreover, the value of buildings and other improvements upon land cannot be assessed with even approximate equality, by the most honest assessors. The value of the rich man's house will inevitably be under-estimated; while the value of the multitude of cheap houses will be relatively, if not actually over-estimated.[1] The tax on improvements, therefore, like that on personal property, is not a really direct tax; and it cannot be fairly apportioned among the taxpayers. These taxes are as bad as a tariff for revenue, because they fall upon consumption and are paid chiefly by the poor; and they are worse than such a tariff, because they cannot be as honestly and efficiently collected.

There is but one reasonable excuse for taxing buildings and improvements upon land, when personal property is not taxed. They cannot run away. All other objections to taxes on visible chattels apply with equal force to taxes on chattels affixed to land.

§ 2. **Tax upon all improvements indirect.** Intelligent residents of cities have so long been accustomed to the idea that taxes upon buildings distribute themselves among tenants, that it will meet with ready acceptance. But when we go further and assert that taxes upon the value of other improvements, and especially upon the

[1] This is true everywhere. But it has been shown, conclusively and in detail, that this unjust discrepancy is carried to an enormous extent in Chicago.

value added to land by cultivation, is not a direct tax, but distributes itself in the same way, the doctrine will be considered novel. The vast majority of farm owners and farm hirers have never thought of such a thing. Yet the one proposition must be as true as the other. Let us candidly inquire into the facts.

Our first inquiry must be into the nature and average value of the class of improvements now referred to, which may perhaps be called "absorbed improvements," since they are so completely absorbed into the land as to be inseparable from it. Buildings can be torn down. Fences can be removed. But the value added by plowing, stubbing, clearing, manuring, pasturing, and cultivation cannot suddenly be taken away. Even fences cannot profitably be carried off; and drains or similar works cannot be removed, although they may be destroyed. The average value of such improvements, entirely exclusive of buildings, is shown to be $40 per acre, in Massachusetts[1]; and it can hardly be less than $20 per acre in any place where the work of cultivation has been thoroughly done.

Dealing first with the case of the tenant, and assuming the improvement of the land to have been made or paid for by the landlord, it would seem to be just as certain that the average rate of interest upon this added value must be paid by the tenant, in addition to the mere ground rent, as that such interest must be paid upon the value of a dwelling-house. For, if all farm tenants combine to refuse such payment, all farm landlords will cease to make such improvements. The process of enforcing payment of this increased rent might be much slower than the like process with respect to buildings; but the end would surely be the same. This being conceded, how could there be any difference with regard to taxes on these

[1] Census 1885; vol. 3, p. xlviii.

improvements? If the landlord had to pay such taxes, without being able to recover them from his tenant, his interest upon the investment would fall below the rate which he could obtain upon other property; and he would cease to invest in farm improvements. Gradually, new tenants would find no improved farms ready for them ; and they would offer to pay taxes and interest on improvements of all kinds. The tenants' supposed combination would thus be broken ; and the tax would be shifted upon all tenants.

Dealing next with the community at large, it would seem obvious that the tax upon such improvements, quite as much as the tax upon factories, mills, or shops, would be ultimately added to the cost of production and would be distributed among the consumers of farm products, just as surely, in the long run, as taxes upon imported goods or home-made whisky. Undoubtedly, it would take a long time to complete the transfer, if taxes upon improvements were newly imposed. But as they have been collected regularly, for time, whereof the memory of man runneth not to the contrary, they are most certainly distributed to-day, with as near an approach to accuracy as any other indirect taxes whatever. If taxes upon consumption are to be got rid of, taxes upon all kinds of improvements of land, which can be ascertained and separately valued, must be abolished.

§ 3. **Taxation of improvements injurious to the public interest.** The taxation of improvements upon land is in many ways attended with injury to the public good. No attempt will be made here to deal with this subject exhaustively. Only a few obvious results will be mentioned.

It has already been pointed out that the tendency of all taxation upon things of human production is to diminish the quantity and degrade the quality of such things. This principle applies to land improvements as much as to movable chattels; and if movables should be relieved from taxation, while fixtures remain subject to it, the weight of taxation upon them would of course be greatly increased; and their production would be more than ever discouraged.

Beautiful buildings are a source of constant instruction and delight. Those who design and erect such buildings, in places where they can be easily seen by multitudes of people, are public benefactors. But beauty in a building attracts the attention of the assessor, and leads to an increase of valuation far in excess of its actual cost. It is no answer to say that the assessor will reduce the assessment, upon evidence that he has overvalued the building. He will not have *over*valued anything. He will simply have *under*valued the ugly buildings more than the handsome ones. The effect will be to increase the burden upon handsome buildings, precisely as much as if they were overvalued, yet without the possibility of a remedy. Thus the taxation of buildings is a constant and severe discouragement to the development of architectural taste and beauty.

§ 4. **Proof from experience.** The mere substitution of good glass for bad, in the front windows of a house, usually leads to an increase of the assessment, to an amount twice or thrice the cost of the improvement, Cases could be given in which the expenditure of $200 in making the front of a house neat and agreeable has been promptly followed by an increase of $2000 in the assessment, thus imposing a permanent fine of 25 per cent. per annum on the cost of the improvement. It is dangerous even to mend a broken gate or repair a rotten front walk. Shrewd house-owners confine most of their improvements to the interior or the rear of their houses, so that the assessor shall not see them, on his annual rounds. There are many houses in large cities, having no external signs of difference, which differ in cost by from $50,000 to $200,000, by reason of interior improvements, which the assessor knows nothing about. Yet if $10,000 had been spent upon the front of one of these houses its assessment would have been increased at least $20,000. The more honest and faithful the assessor may be, the worse will be his work in such cases.

Nor is it merely in matters of taste and beauty that the system works evil. Houses are cramped and badly built, in order to avoid taxation. In the city of Brooklyn, thousands of houses have three full stories in the rear, but only two and a half in front, for no other reason than that, by the custom of assessors, such houses are charged as only two-storied houses, thus reducing taxation upon them 20 or 30 per cent. below three-storied houses on the same block. Old, decayed, and unhealthy houses are patched up for years, simply because if they were completely rebuilt the tax upon them would be increased to such an extent as to destroy all the profit. We reproduce, at the verge of the twentieth century, the absurd oppressions of the thirteenth, when every rich Jew kept the front of his house filthy and broken down, so as to deceive his Gentile plunderers, while indulging in magnificence in the secrecy of his inner rooms.

The same thing is true in rural districts. A farmer who ventures to beautify the outside of his house, to build a model barn or stable, to make his fence an ornament, instead of a nuisance, or even to make his lawn and garden beautiful or his farm neat, must expect to pay a large fine for his rash act. He is treated worse than a criminal; for if he had committed a crime he would be fined only once in his life for one act; but if he has dared to beautify his house and farm he must pay a new fine for every year of his life; and his heirs must go on paying it forever. The virtues of the father are visited in penalties upon the children to the third and fourth generation.[1]

§ 5. Just and equal assessments impracticable.

Justice and equality in the assessment of buildings and other improvements of land are nearly as impracticable as in the case of ordinary visible chattels. The most honest assessors cannot appraise them with even a reasonable approximation to equality. This can be proved both by theory and by experience.

The value of a dwelling-house, for example, cannot be fairly decided by any outside inspection. In cities nothing is more common than to find houses almost precisely alike in outside appearance, which differ greatly in comfort, luxury, and market price. One is well built; the other is not. One is warm in winter, and cool in summer; the next house is the reverse. One has well arranged rooms; the other has not. One is simple externally, but has an interior air of comfort, which makes it always salable; its next neighbor has precisely the same outside, but is so unhomelike, that it gives one a chill to cross its threshold. One has a plain and unattractive interior; the next house is permanently decorated with magnificence and taste. One is decorated with a sham magnifi-

---

[1] Mr. Wells's famous Report on Local Taxation (1871) contains some admirable illustrations on this point. He mentions instances in which every improvement made upon a railroad was made an excuse for a great increase in its taxes, to the plain discouragement of such improvements and to the peril of human life. He tells how, after the building of one handsome railway station, on the New York Central Railroad, had been punished by a heavy tax, Mr. Vanderbilt refused to build any more new depots. The hideous structures which still remain at Buffalo and other important stations, are a continuing testimony to the folly of taxing new buildings.

cence, which would cause any assessor, if admitted to inspect it, to put a high value upon it. Another is adorned with such perfect simplicity and harmonious beauty as to cost and be salable for twice as much ; yet no assessor would ever guess it.

These are not imaginary cases ; they are illustrations taken from a multitude which have come under the writer's own observation. Houses could easily be pointed out, in large cities, which are assessed at about the same value, and which present substantially the same external appearance, but which differ in cost by $50,000, $100,000, and even $250,000. Probably this entire difference would not be realized upon a sale ; but a large part of it certainly would be.

§ 6. **The wealthy relieved : the poor burdened.** It follows that the dwellings of the very rich will inevitably be assessed, by an honest and unprejudiced assessor, at much less, in proportion to their real value, than the dwellings of those in moderate circumstances. As a matter of course a dishonest assessor will value rich men's houses at still lower rates ; because it is from rich men that bribes can be most easily obtained. In any event, the most valuable houses in cities are sure to escape their full share of taxation.

This, again, is no mere theory. It is a notorious fact. A recent investigation, conducted by a fearless and impartial journal in Chicago, has demonstrated this fact, so far as that city is concerned, in great detail and with conclusive proof. This inequality of assessment is carried to such an enormous extent in Chicago as to leave no room for doubt that it is largely due to actual bribery. But it is found (in a much less degree) in cities where not the slightest suspicion attaches to assessors.

Precisely the same thing is true with respect to office buildings, mills, factories, and all other buildings used for business purposes in large cities. It has been matter of common rumor and universal belief in one such city, that the office of assessor, in one small ward, full of great office buildings, was worth $75,000 a year to its occupant.

§ 7. Farmers unequally burdened. What buildings are likely to be assessed with reasonable equality, as compared with each other? Can there be any doubt that they are farm buildings and village dwellings? Among these, substantial uniformity of style and cost prevails. The difference will be, for the most part, a matter of a few hundred dollars. Interior decorations are unknown. But, whatever variations there may be, all are familiarly known to the whole neighborhood. The village assessor usually knows all about them; and, if he does not, he has only to ask a few questions at the village store.

The consequence is that with respect to improvements upon land just as much as with respect to personal property, farmers and villagers are sure to be taxed more fully and accurately than the residents of cities; while the richest city residents will pay the smallest share of the tax, in proportion to the value of their property.

The full effect of the taxation of improvements upon farmers and other residents of rural districts must, however, be reserved for a later chapter, dealing with affirmative propositions. Up to this point, our work is purely negative. The example of Nature herself has been followed. We have been engaged in finding out what is bad, not in determining what is good. That is next to be undertaken.

CHAPTER IX.

THE NATURAL TAX.

§ 1. **Automatic taxation.** Having seen that every form of indirect taxation is unjust to the poor, and that every form of so-called direct taxation thus far examined is unjust to the honest, we cannot be surprised at the unanimity with which it has hitherto been declared that there is no scientific or natural method of taxation.

Nevertheless, if we can find in actual operation, in every civilized country, a species of taxation which automatically collects from every citizen an amount almost exactly proportioned to the fair and full market value of the benefits which he derives from the government under which he lives and the society which surrounds him, may we not safely infer that this is natural taxation? And is not such taxation capable of being reduced to a science?

Such an automatic, irresistible, and universal system does exist. All over the world men pay to a superior authority a tribute, proportioned with wonderful exactness to these social advantages. Each man is compelled to do this, by the fact that other men surround him, eager to pay tribute in his place if he will not. The just amount of this tribute is determined by the competition of all his neighbors; who calculate to a dollar just how much the privilege is worth to them, and who will gladly take his place and pay in his stead. Every man must, therefore, pay as much as some other man will give for his place; and no man can be made to pay any more.

§ 2. Ground rent. This tribute is sometimes paid to the state, when it is called a tax; but it is far more often paid to private individuals, when it is called ground rent.

Where there is no government there is no ground rent. As government grows more complex and does more for society, ground rents increase. Any advantage possessed by one piece of land over another will, it is true, give rise to rent; but that rent cannot be collected without the aid of government; and no advantage in fertility is ever equal in value to the advantage of society and government. An acre of sand on the coast of New Jersey, at Atlantic City, Cape May, or Long Branch, is worth more rent than a million acres of fertile land five hundred miles distant from all human society. The sixteenth of an acre of bare rock in New York City is worth more than a thousand acres of the best farming land in Manitoba.

Ground rent, therefore, is the tribute which natural laws levy upon every occupant of land, as the market price of all the social as well as natural advantages appertaining to that land, including, necessarily, his just share of the cost of government.[1]

---

[1] The definition of rent here given is not inconsistent with the principles of Ricardo; although it is not expressed in his words. As Senior and other friends of Ricardo have remarked, he never took pains to express himself accurately; and he constantly assumed that his readers would remember every limitation which he had once laid down and would comprehend all that was implied in his mind. His definition of the law of Rent is a remarkable illustration of his peculiar methods.

No man could have been more fully aware than was Ricardo, of the enormous amount of rent which was collected in his own time from land which had no fertility and no productive power. Most of his life was spent upon just such land in London; and for the use of such land he paid and received great rents. Yet his famous definition assumes that rent is never paid for anything except "the use of the original and indestructible powers of

§ 3. **The justice of ground rent.** Now observe how perfectly this natural tribute meets all the requirements of abstract justice, with which our professor-friends have so long wrestled in vain. Here is the exact *quid pro quo.* No sane man, in any ordinary society, pays too much rent. For he pays no more than some other man is willing to pay for the same privileges. He therefore pays no more than the market value of the advantage which he gains over other men by occupying that precise position on the earth. He gains a certain profit out of that position, which he could not gain elsewhere. That

the soil." And his exposition of the operation of this law is confined so strictly to the growth of "corn" (that is, wheat) that some of his disciples and many of his critics seriously assume that Ricardo did not suspect the existence of any law of rent, which was not governed entirely by the growth of "corn."

But Ricardo's methods, in this and in other instances, recall the style of the Ten Commandments. Taken literally, those commandments are as defective a code of morals as can be found in almost any ethical system. They do not in terms forbid the most brutal violence or recklessness, if death does not result, nor any form of fraud or swindling not amounting to literal theft. They do not forbid any form of outrage upon unmarried women. They do not forbid lying, except in judicial proceedings. They have not a word about malice, envy, hatred, bribery, betrayal of trust, or even treason. And yet both the Hebrew nation and the Christian church have always seen these prohibitions implied in the curt words which denounce merely a few of the worst and most striking forms of crime.

So it is with Ricardo. He took the most striking and easily understood illustration of a principle, as his method of stating the principle itself. His writings always bear the marks of a genius, which was driven by its own internal energy to find relief in utterance, but which cared very little whether its utterances were understood or not. In this particular instance, he suggested a principle by a single illustration of the most familiar character. But the principle is not limited by the illustration. Any advantage which one piece of land has over another, for the use of man, was included, in Ricardo's mind, among the "original and indestructible powers of the soil." And foremost among these advantages stands that of affording standing ground, in the midst of a highly civilized society, under the protection of a highly organized and faithful government.

fact is conclusive proof that this profit is not the fruit of his labor, but comes out of some superior fertility in the soil, some superior opportunity for selling the fruits of his labor, some superior protection from government in the enjoyment of those fruits, or some other advantage of mere position. Thus he receives full value, in exchange for his payment. *He* receives it; not merely society in general. He receives the *whole* of it: he is not compelled to divide a dollar's worth of this benefit with his neighbors. But, on the other hand, he pays the full value of what he thus receives; and he owes nothing more to anybody. The transaction is closed, upon fair and equal terms.

Here, then, is a tax, just, equal, full, fair, paid for full value received, returning full value for the payment, meeting all the requirements of that ideal tax, which professors and practical men alike have declared to be an impossibility. It is not merely a tax which justice *allows;* it is one which justice *demands.* It is not merely one which *ought* to be collected: it is one which infallibly will be and *is* collected. It is not merely one which the state *ought* to see collected; it is one which, in the long run, the state *cannot prevent* from being collected. The state can change the particular landlord: it cannot abolish rent.

§ 4. **Landlords natural tax-gatherers.** It is quite true that some men do not pay ground rent to any one else. But these are landlords, of the most highly developed type. A few of these men seem, at first glance, neither to pay nor receive ground rent. But this is an illusion. They do receive such rent, in the value which remains in their possession, in excess of what they would hold if they paid rent like other people. Moreover, such men almost invariably have either paid a price for the land on which they live (which is capitalized rent paid by them), or they hold land which cost them less than they could sell it for (which is capitalized rent gained by them), or they have done both.

Those who actually receive ground rent, or who could receive it if they would, form the class which we call "landlords." They are the tax-gatherers appointed by Nature. Year by year they assess the value of the privilege of occupying their land. They can do this, with an accuracy to which no government assessor can ever attain; because they receive, at least once a year, the best possible information as to this value, in the form of bids from tenants. They have only to announce their willingness to receive bids; and the bids come in. Nobody runs after the assessor, to tell him what property is worth. Everybody runs after the landlord, to tell him what his land is worth. Not that everybody tells him the truth; but he soon finds out what is the truth, by comparing conflicting statements.

The landlord, we repeat, is Nature's elected tax-gatherer. But Nature does not compel him, any more than any other collector of taxes, to pay over to the state what he collects. This must be done by the state itself.

§ 5. **Taxation of ground rents.** Nature, having thus provided a method by which all men pay, of necessity, a tribute sufficient to defray all expenses of government, clearly points to the collection of such expenses from this tribute. We have already seen that Nature and Science condemn every other method of raising public revenue, by making equality and justice impossible under any such method. Do they not, with equal clearness and precision, point to the taxation of ground rents, as not merely a just method of raising revenue, but also as the *only* just one? Scientifically speaking, a tax upon ground rents is not a tax at all: it is merely the collection, by the state, of a tax already levied by an automatic process. If we call it a tax, it is a tax upon the proceeds of taxation, and nothing else. Until this source of revenue is exhausted, every other tax is double taxation. So long as this fund remains, every other tax is of necessity unjust, as truly as it would be unjust to squander the proceeds of any tax among a few favored officials and then levy the whole of the same tax over again upon the people. Seldom has there been a more beautiful illustration of the wise yet relentless working of natural law, than in the proved impossibility of justly collecting any tax other than upon ground rent. It shows that Nature makes it impossible to execute justly a statute which is in its nature unjust. The propriety of an exclusive tax upon ground rents is established, not merely by affirmative proof of its justice, but by the demonstration of universal experience that no other form of taxation can be made effective, adequate, just, and equal.

§ 6. **No objectionable methods of collection.** The absolute soundness of the theory upon which the tax on ground rents is based is further established by the fact that its efficient collection requires no objectionable methods. Such a tax already exists in the United States; although it is covered up by a multitude of other taxes. We all know, by experience, that such a tax is entirely free from the oppressive and corrupting incidents of other taxes. It calls for no personal returns, no taxpayers' oaths, no exposure of private affairs. The collector of such a tax would not have the slightest excuse for inquisitorial proceedings, for the examination of private books, for entry into houses, for personal searches, or for asking a single question of the taxpayer. In fact, he would not pay the smallest attention to any statement which a taxpayer might make. Women and children would be taxed no more heavily than men. Trust estates would pay no more than others. There would be no exemptions, no favoritism, and no preference given, either to the rich or to the poor. Mistakes of course would occur; and the bribery of assessors would be possible. But those are an extremely small part of the evils of all existing methods of taxation; and some of the most monstrous inequalities are found where the assessors are absolutely incorruptible and thoroughly competent. All of these would disappear.

§ 7. **Assessment of ground rent practicable.** It is asserted by a few persons, who have given no careful consideration to the subject, that it is as difficult to assess accurately the value of the bare land, as it is to assess any other property. This objection will not bear the least examination.

Of course *absolute* accuracy is not to be expected in anything. It has not pleased God to make this world literally perfect, in any respect; and man cannot hope to be wiser than his Maker. But a close approach to accuracy is possible in taxing ground rents; and it is not possible in any other tax.

Where land is rented separately from its improvements, the tax can be collected with almost ideal accuracy. The tenant can be required to pay it, being allowed to deduct it from his rent. He will have no motive for understating the rent; and if he overstates it, the loss will be his own. Nothing but positive fraud on the part of the official assessor can produce inequality in this tax; and such fraud would be too dangerous to be common.

Where land and improvements are rented together, the value of the land alone is always approximately ascertainable. Real estate dealers in the district would have little difficulty in estimating the price at which any tract of land could readily be sold ; and this would be the proper basis for assessment.

Where land is owned by the actual occupier, dealers can still easily estimate its market value. Titles to town lots are continually changing ; thus fixing a standard of prices: while in rural districts there is much less variation in prices; and all the neighbors know the relative value of each farm. Whatever inequalities might remain, it is certain that they would be vastly less than those which are now common.

§ 8. **Assessment of farm lands.** It has been asked: How can the unimproved value of farm lands be ascertained, after they have been cleared, ploughed, drained, and fertilized for many years? The answer is simple. The whole of a farm is to be assessed at the same value, per acre, which attaches to the unimproved land, remaining on the farm and having substantially the same natural advantages or disadvantages. It is next asked: How shall such an estimate be made, if the whole farm has been fully cultivated? There is no such farm, except a few very small ones, selected from larger farms ; and in those cases the valuation can be made upon the basis of unimproved land on adjoining farms. It has been pretended that there are cases, in which there is no unimproved land near by. But this is almost absurd. Yet if such a marvellous farm could be found, it is certain to be close to a highway. The price which could be obtained for the land covered by the highway, if closed and sold, would afford a perfect test of the value of all adjoining land.

But the best reply to all such objections is to be found in the practical experience of California, where this very method of assessment is carried out in agricultural districts, without difficulty, having been required by law, ever since 1879, and by the experience of Massachusetts, where the value of farm lands has been ascertained by the decennial census, for many years, carefully separating the value of improved lands from unimproved and unimprovable lands.

§ 9. **Judicial correction of assessments.** Under the present systems of taxation, it has been found necessary to allow appeals to the courts from some unjust assessments : while State boards of equalization in New York, Illinois, California, and other States put county valuations up or down, in order to remedy the evils caused by local carelessness or evasion. These remedies should be extended and placed upon a foundation of complete justice. The courts should be given full power to make local assessments uniform, reducing every assessment to the basis of the lowest in the county. The county would lose no revenue ; for the tax rate would be increased to correspond with the general reduction. But citizens would be relieved from the gross injustice which many now suffer. At present, in New York, if not everywhere, a taxpayer can obtain no relief, unless his own property is overvalued. But an undervaluation of his neighbors is just as effectual an increase of his share of the general burden as would be an overvaluation of his own property. It would cast an offensive responsibility upon him, to give him relief only through a judgment increasing his neighbors assessments ; and such a course would produce no better result for the county than would a general reduction to one common basis. The State at large would take care of its interest in the matter, through the board of equalization.

§ 10. **Correction by sales.** If all other remedies failed, one would remain, which is far too dangerous for use under existing methods, but which would be quite safe under the new system. The owner of any real estate which was assessed for more than the real value of the bare land, could refuse to pay the tax. Then his land would be offered for sale to the highest bidder, subject to the obligation of paying to the owner the appraised value of all improvements thereon, upon the principles already stated. The value could never be more than the cost of replacing the improvements, and it would often be much less; because costly buildings are frequently erected in situations where they are or become useless, and therefore of no value. To the full extent of their actual market value, however, the purchaser at a tax sale would be required to indemnify the owner. Such a sale would determine the precise value of the land, for the purposes of taxation.

Nor would such sales, however frequent they might be, work any hardship to the landowner. He would have a right to bid; and he would have great advantages over any other bidder. All the money paid in excess of the tax and the penalty would go directly into his pocket; and, therefore, he would be the only bidder not required to pay more than that sum. If the tax were really excessive no one would bid up to it; because the purchaser would be compelled to pay annually thereafter as large a tax as he was willing to bid at the sale. The tax sale, in short, would fix the valuation upon which future assessments would be made. Thus the ground rent (which, capitalized, constitutes the only value of any land) would be fully taxed; while the land-owner would have absolute security for the possession of the value of all his improvements, free of tax. But no such experiment would ever become really necessary.

§ 11. **Taxation of franchises and monopolies.** It has been already mentioned that the professed defenders of farmers and other owners of small homesteads oppose the concentration of taxation upon ground rents, on the plea that this would exempt all franchises and monopolies, including railways, express companies, telegraphs, telephones, gasworks, electric lighting works, oil-pipe lines, and the like. If this were the fact we may be sure that the shrewd managers of such monopolies, assisted as they are by the most sagacious and experienced advisers in the country, would have discovered it by this time. We may also be sure that the legislatures of two thirds of the States, owned as they are, body and soul, by corporations of this precise class, would hasten to avow their conversion to the principle of taxing ground rents and to embody it in their statutes. The Senate of the United States would before now have passed any necessary amendment to the Constitution, by a two-third vote.

But do we see the slightest tendency in this direction? Is the proposal received with favor by the managers of a single great railway or telegraph or of any great monopoly? On the contrary, is it not notorious that they are unanimously and bitterly opposed to it?

These gentlemen are not deceived. They know well enough that their valuable franchises represent exclusive rights to the use of land, and that they neither have nor can have any exclusive rights to anything else, except to patent rights, which are very costly, and which last only for a few years.

§ 12. **Railway franchises.** Take one of our great railway lines, for example. Add up either the market value or the cost of replacing its rails, equipment, building improvements and chattels of every kind, whether movable or immovable, and at a most liberal valuation. The total will not come within millions of its nominal debt, and will never touch its capital stock. What gives value to the enormous amount of stock? The exclusive privilege of using a narrow strip of barren land, five hundred, a thousand, or two thousand miles long, unbroken by highways or any other rights over land, whether public or private. Under the present system railway managers persuade local assessors that this land should be valued no higher than equally barren land in adjoining farms; and the farmers' especial advocates insist that this is the true basis of valuation. But it is absurd.

The value of all land depends upon the value of the use which can be made of it. No farmer can use his land for the carriage of goods or passengers, beyond the limits of his own farm. If all the farmers between New York and San Francisco agreed to build a railway, without forming a railway corporation, they would be compelled to break their line at every highway, to dismount their passengers and to unload their freight. Therefore, nobody outside of a railway company can use his land for this most valuable purpose. And this privilege of using an unbroken strip of land, with locomotives running forty miles an hour, is all which gives to the stock of any American railway company its market value; while it generally covers from one third to one half of its bonds, in addition.

The notion that such privileges on land are to be appraised by the acre, like farm lands, can be readily tested by applying the same principle to any other land. In great cities land is often sold at a price estimated by the square foot. Some lots, containing 2000 square feet, are salable for $2,000,000, or $100 per foot. But if a single foot of this land were sold by itself, with the knowledge that no more could be had, who would give even one dollar for it, except as a means of blackmailing the owner of the rest? Just so, the value of a strip of land unbroken for a thousand miles, for use as a railway, is something immense; while the same land cut up in a thousand sections, never to be united, would be almost valueless. For purposes of transportation it would have no value whatever.

Again, the value of land depends upon the variety of uses to which it may lawfully be put. Steam railways, although very useful, are to some extent a nuisance. The government cannot permit them to be operated upon every tract of land. Consequently land owned by individuals is generally restricted to other uses; and it is therefore worth less than land owned by railway companies.

§ 13 **Other franchises.** The franchise of a telegraph company is of the same nature. It is absolutely nothing but an exclusive privilege to extend its wires over land. But this is a privilege of enormous value. The founders of the Western Union Telegraph Company have managed to sell this privilege to investors in its stock, for at least $50,000,000.

The franchises of gas companies, electric light companies, steam heating companies, water works, and the like, consist so obviously of mere privileges to use unimproved land as to need no explanation. Street railroads, also, so palpably own no privileges, other than the mere right to run over bare land, that it seems almost an insult to the understanding of any reader to explain the case. None of these corporations have any other franchises, than these rights over land. For these franchises, most of them have paid enormous bribes to legislators and aldermen. Upon these franchises they have issued vast amounts of stock and bonds. One such corporation, after purchasing all the rails, equipment, and other productions of human labor connected with the road, for about $200,000, proceeded to issue $8,000,000 of stock and bonds, upon its land privileges.

It will be said that there are general railway laws, so

that anybody can construct a new rival line, and thus destroy the land values of an existing line. Whenever that can really be done, the truth of this theory is promptly proved, by the destruction of stock values in both corporations, as in the desperate struggle between the New York Central and the West Shore lines, in 1884 But this is only partially true. A rival line must run through towns and very near cities; or it can get little business. The aldermen of every city must be bought up; and as the old corporation will pay liberal bribes to induce the aldermen to do nothing, the new one must bring far more liberal considerations to bear upon our patriotic rulers. Nor is it merely a question of money. Bribery must be conducted decently and in order. Public sentiment must be judiciously worked up to support the scheme. It requires an immense amount of ingenious and well directed effort to carry any such project into effect.

In the case of street railroads, telegraphic subways, gasworks, and other privileges in cities, it is obvious that the limit is soon reached; and even the liberality of a legislature or a board of aldermen cannot make room for many rival schemes of this kind. The streets cannot be torn up forever; although, in New York and Brooklyn, they do not fall much short of this. The limits imposed by nature are such that more than three fourths of the whole market values of the stock and bonds of corporations, having these municipal privileges, consist of pure land values.

Under the present system, in most cases, all these enormous values go untaxed. The law of New York distinctly exempts franchises from taxation; although it is well settled that they would be taxable as "land" but for this legislative interference. Under the system here proposed all these values would be fairly taxed.

§ 14. **Can the rent tax be shifted?** While the Duke of Argyll and all his landlord allies rend the air with their denunciations of the proposed tax on rent, as confiscation and robbery, other opponents of the tax, appreciating the fact that tenants far out-number landlords at the polls, devote their energy to proving that this tax would all be shifted upon tenants, by an increase of rent, so that landlords would finally pay none of it. If this were true, then no relief from the unequal distribution of wealth can be had; for all direct taxes would ultimately fall upon consumption, just as surely as do indirect taxes. In short, *no* tax would be really direct. The greatest benefit thus far held out, as the result of adopting an exclusive tax upon ground rent, would be unattainable under that or any other system.

On the other hand, if this doctrine is true, the indignation of the Duke of Argyll and all the great landlords of Great Britain and Ireland is absurdly misdirected. If they can recover this tax from their tenants, precisely as the importer of foreign goods recovers customs taxes from the purchasers of those goods, they will lose nothing by the change, and may even profit by it. It is very clear that the landlords do not believe a word of this doctrine of shifting taxation; for if they did they would look with indifference, if not with positive favor, upon the taxation of ground rents. So far from doing this, dukes, earls, and marquises are eagerly struggling in England for election as councilmen and aldermen, for the sole purpose of preventing the taxation of ground rents.

The weight of authority upon such a question is worthy of attention, although by no means decisive. Now, while a few respectable and sincere students of economic science hold to the doctrine of the transferability of the ground-rent tax to the tenants, no one will dispute that an overwhelming weight of authority, both in numbers and in reputation, scout that doctrine as absurd. Not only the entire school of Ricardo and Mill, but also nine tenths or more of other economic writers make it a fundamental doctrine of their science that such a tax never can be transferred to tenants.

§ 15. **The question illustrated.** Let us, however, consider the question for ourselves, as if it were entirely new. The simplest way of testing it is to imagine that the tax was made heavy enough to absorb the whole rent. For, although this is impossible, it really makes no difference whether half or the whole of rent is taken by taxation, so long as the state is determined to take some fixed proportion of rent. Any good accountant can satisfy himself that the result would be the same under either plan. But persons unaccustomed to figures could not follow any other calculation so easily as they can follow one based upon a tax equal to the whole rent.

Let us then suppose the "single tax unlimited" to be in operation. Let us suppose the total ground rent of the United States to be $1,000,000,000. The total production of the nation does not exceed $13,000,000,000 per annum. Out of this, 65,000,000 people have to draw their living expenses. Even if they had no ground rent and no taxes to pay they could not possibly save $5,000,000,000 a year. But suppose they could. The landlords collect in rent $1,000,000,000. The government takes the whole of this in taxes. The landlords then shift the tax upon the tenants, and insist upon collecting $2,000,000,000 in rent. But the government next year taxes the whole of this increased sum out of the landlords. The landlords then raise their rent to $3,000,000,000. But the government immediately takes the whole of that in taxes. The landlords raise their rent to $4,000,000,000. The government again takes it all. They raise rent once more to $5,000,000,000. Again it is all swallowed up in taxes. Will the landlords raise their rent again? How can they? They would by that time have taken every dollar that tenants earned, over the barest living; and if they attempted to extort another dollar, some tenant would die of starvation; and rents would fall, from lack of tenants. And as the government would have extracted the whole of their rent, they would have gained not a dollar by their persistent oppression of their tenants.

§ 16. **Distinction between land and houses.** It will be said that nothing of this kind could really be done by any government. Quite true; but that is simply because nothing of the kind could be done by landlords. Landlords know, to their cost, that it takes three or four years to enable them to recover from tenants even increased taxation upon *houses;* although they will recover it in the end. But, since it is difficult to recover a tax which tends to diminish the number of houses, how vastly more difficult must it be to recover a tax upon the value of land, which has no tendency whatever to diminish the amount of available land.

And here the reader can see the reason for the distinction. If owners of houses cannot recover from tenants the tax upon houses, nobody will build any more houses for renting. But the owner of land cannot create any more land, no matter how liberally he may be paid for it; and he cannot diminish the area of land, no matter how little he may receive for it. Every increase of taxation upon ground rents makes it more difficult to keep land out of use; and therefore it increases the competition between landlords to get tenants. Under a light tax upon ground rents, two tenants pursue one landlord. But under a heavy tax, two landlords pursue one tenant. If ground rents should be taxed even to half their amount, landlords without tenants would be compelled to sell at any price to other landlords who could get tenants. The tendency of all taxes upon ground rents, therefore, is to reduce rent, rather than to increase it; and this makes the very idea of a transfer of such taxes to the tenant utterly absurd.

A moment's reflection will satisfy every one that landlords charge just as much for their land as they can possibly get, except in special cases of good nature, charity, or ignorance.[1] In all ordinary cases the only reason why they do not charge more is that they cannot find anybody able and willing to pay more. How can this condition be changed by taxes upon rent? It is not and it cannot be. The average landlord will charge the highest rent which he can get, tax or no tax. And, as no man will ever get more than he *can* get, no amount of tax upon ground rents will ever be shifted over to tenants by an increase of rents.

§ 17. **Amount of the tax on rent.** It does not follow that the state should compel the landlord to pay over all that he receives. If the state could and should do this, the landlord would cease to do his work; because he would receive no compensation for it. Natural laws again settle this question, by making such exact collection impossible. Not all the power of all governments, concentrated upon the landlords of a single town, could extract from them

---

[1] This is universally true in the United States. In many parts of Europe, especially in England, agricultural rents are limited by custom and public opinion. In Ireland, they are often limited by law. But all that results from such restrictions is that rent is divided between two or more landlords. The mass of the people, who are the real, final tenants, gain nothing whatever. The farm-tenant either sublets the farm, at a higher rent, or he makes a larger profit out of the farm, without selling his produce any cheaper or paying a penny more wages to his laborers.

precisely one hundred per cent. of the rent received by them.

Nor does it follow that even ninety per cent. of rent ought to be taken. Where rents are large the retention of ten or even five per cent. might be sufficient to induce landlords to follow up tenants and extract from them that just rent which every one ought to pay. Where rents are small a commission of ten or even fifteen per cent. may be insufficient for this purpose. An iron rule is not a natural rule ; and it will not work well.

What would Nature or Science dictate upon this point? Is it not that the state should collect from the natural tax collectors whatever amount the state really needs, for the effective but economical administration of government? Is it not better, in case there should remain any considerable excess over this, that it should remain in private hands, rather than it should be taken by the state, before the state officers know how to use it for the real benefit of the people at large? Grant, if you please, that there would be such surplus of rent as to breed wasteful luxury among landlords, is not this less injurious to the community than wholesale waste and embezzlement of public funds? Our whole national history illustrates the truth that surplus public revenues first corrupt public officers and then debauch the nation itself.

But in fact, in the long run, there will be no such question to decide. The honest needs of public government grow faster than population and fully as fast as wealth itself. Local taxation will increase rapidly ; and it ought to do so. Such taxation increased in Ohio, for example, 1400 per cent. in forty years, between 1846 and 1886 ; while population increased only 100 per cent. and wealth 1000 per cent. It is more likely that vigilance will be needed to prevent the taxation of rent from rising too fast, than that it would be required to keep landlords from retaining too much. This does not imply that ground rent will not be sufficient to supply many, possibly all, of those additions to human happiness which Henry George has pictured in such glowing words. But such extensions of the sphere of government must take place gradually ; or they will be ruinous failures, simply because the state cannot at once furnish the necessary machinery for their successful operation.

This natural tax might be adopted in one day, not only without injury to the nation, but with positive benefit to more than nine tenths of all the people. But this would be strictly upon condition that the amount collected for public use should not at first exceed that which was previously collected. Indeed, it would be essential to the permanence of such taxation that public revenues should be at the beginning of the new system even smaller than they were immediately before. And we may be perfectly sure that they would be. A body of 4,000,000 taxpayers will take care of that.

§ 18. **New benefits shared with landlords.** There is, nevertheless, a certain element of truth underlying the idea that a rent-tax can be shifted. While it is not true that one dollar of the tax can be transferred to the tenant, in any case where rent is fixed upon strictly business principles, it is true that, in many places, and especially in rural districts of England, the owners of farm lands do not charge the full market value of the land to their tenants. Personal considerations, kindness of feeling, custom, long-continued relations between the families of the landlord and the tenant, public opinion, tradition, the desire to control votes, and many similiar influences keep rents below their market value. Under a system of taxation, concentrated upon rents, these influences would lose much of their power. Under a tax, deliberately raised to the highest practicable point, these influences would lose *all* of their power. Tenants would, therefore, find their rents increased to the full value of the land. Here would seem to be a real shifting of the tax.

But this would be only a seeming, not a reality. The tenants, who now receive the benefit of those influences, are in reality themselves landlords, to that extent. They divide economic rent with their landlords. They do not divide the rent, thus left in their pockets, with the community at large. They do not reduce the prices of their products or charge any less for their services. Many of them sublet a part of the land to others, to whom they charge the full market price. The community, as a whole, pays just as much rent, when the duke allows the farmer to occupy land at 20 per cent. below its full value, as it does when the duke's creditors seize his land and make the farmer pay the last penny that the land is worth. The farmer sells wheat at the same price and pays to his laborers the same wages, in either case. But there is a good deal of difference in the style of his daughters' dresses and the length of his annual vacation.

There is another result which must follow, if the community gains in wealth and happiness, through this change in methods of taxation. Every advance in prosperity— every widespread increase in wealth, tends to increase rent. If it is true, as will be presently maintained, that this reform in taxation will stimulate production, increase wages, promote the development of industry, add to the profits of capital and reward the efforts of skill, then there will be a greatly increased demand for the locations which offer the best natural opportunities for the use of capital, labor and skill; and ground rents will rise. But this is not the shifting of an old burden; it is the sharing of a new benefit.

CHAPTER X.

ONE TAX ENOUGH.

§ 1. Adverse statements considered. Is this one tax enough? Can all the needs of government be supplied by a tax upon ground rent alone?

Ambitious philosophers, on both sides of the Atlantic, have convinced themselves that in no country is economic rent (the annual value of land alone) large enough to pay even the existing taxes. This assumption was first brought forward to serve as an argument in England, with an air of triumph which has seduced American philosophers into reliance upon the same theory. It was asserted by Mr. W. H. Mallock and others, with the utmost confidence, that the whole rental of Great Britain and Ireland would not suffice, within many million pounds, to pay the existing annual taxes, national and local. This assertion was supported by a bristling array of figures, not in round numbers, but with an impressive detail, implying absolute accuracy. We need not imitate this pretended accuracy, but may concede that the average British and Irish taxes, imperial and local, for several years past (excluding, of course, postal and telegraph revenues, etc.) have amounted to about £118,000,000 sterling. Mr. Mallock calls the total rental of land in Great Britain and Ireland £99,000,000.[1]

[1] *Property and Progress*, p. 114.

Professor William T. Harris improves upon Mr. Mallock, and states the annual rent of all land in Great Britain and Ireland at £65,442,000 (*Forum*, July, 1887).

Mr. George Gunton (*Forum*, March, 1887) presents, with "crushing" confidence, a third and entirely different statement of British and Irish rents, fixing them, with mathematical accuracy, at £131,468,288; being double the estimate of Professor Harris and nearly one third more than that of Mr. Mallock.

It is obvious that all these learned philosophers cannot be right; and therefore it is not surprising to find that all of them are wrong. What *is* surprising is that their errors are so enormous, that they are caused by the use of second-hand authorities, yet could not have been made if even those authorities had been read with ordinary care, and that they prove an entire ignorance of the subject treated.

All of their figures are absurdly erroneous. All of these gentlemen have used tables which *excluded every penny of rent collected in the city of London!* All of them have excluded the value of land in railways, canals, mines, etc. Mr. Mallock further excludes all the rent of Scotland and Ireland. Prof. Harris caps the climax, by excluding the rent of all land not used for farming or similar rural purposes!

When a city population of over 4,000,000 pay no rent, and when houses, railways, canals, gasworks, and mines can hang in the air without earthly support, these statistics may have some value, but not until then.

§ 2. **Mr. Atkinson on Boston rents.** Space would fail to enumerate all the professors, doctors of philosophy, editors, and essayists who have followed the same line of argument in America, and have demonstrated, to their own satisfaction, that American ground rents could never suffice to meet the necessary burdens of taxation. One example will suffice for all; and a quotation from Mr. Edward Atkinson (*Forum*, February, 1889) will cover all that has been said by any one on that side. He says:

"It is also probably an error to suppose that the present rental value of land, taken by itself, including that somewhat indefinite factor, the so-called 'unearned increment,' even if it could all be converted to public use in payment of taxes, would suffice to meet the necessary expenses of government even for state, city, and town purposes. For several years the assessors of the city of Boston, where the present valuation of land is very high, have kept the valuation of land for the purpose of taxation, separate from that of buildings and personal property. The valuation of the city for the year 1888 was $764,000,000, on which a tax is to be assessed of $10,000,000 for city, county, and state purposes, at the rate of $13.50 on each $1000 worth of property. Land and buildings are assessed nearly if not quite up to the market value. Personal property is reached by the assessors of the city of Boston in larger measure than in any other city in the country. At the average of recent years, the value of land is $333,000,000; of buildings and improvements, $230,000,000; of personal property, $201,000,000. In order to raise $10,000,000 revenue the tax upon the whole must be $13.50 on each $1000. If the assessment were made upon real estate, including land and buildings, the rate would be $17.75; or, making allowance for abatements, $18.50. If assessed on land value only, the assessment would be a little over $33, allowing for abatements about $35, on each $1000. It is doubtful if the rental now obtained by the owners of all the land of Boston would more than meet the $10,000,000 expenses of the state and city, omitting wholly the amount required by the nation. It must be remembered that our national taxes amount to a sum as large, if not larger, than all the state, county, city, and town taxes combined."

A close examination of all figures of this kind would disclose a great undervaluation of land, arising from the universal practice of assessors to rate vacant land held for speculative purposes, much lower than occupied land having precisely similar market value. But we should be so grateful to our opponents for condescending to drop into figures of any kind, as to accept Mr. Atkinson's statistics without troublesome criticism. For these figures, incorrect as they are, nevertheless fully suffice to refute the argument which they are brought forward to support.

§ 3. **What the critics have overlooked.** All critics of this class have overlooked the transparent fact that ground rent already bears a certain proportion of taxation, and that when it is proposed to put all taxes upon rent, the taxes now borne by rent must be deducted from the total amount, before reckoning the amount which would be cast upon rent by such a change in taxation.

They have also overlooked the equally obvious fact that the market price of land is always reduced by the capitalized value of the taxes already upon it. For the price of land being nothing more than the capitalized value of the *net* rent which can be derived from it, that value is invariably as much smaller, in proportion to the value which it would have if untaxed, as the net rent is smaller than the gross rent.

To illustrate: If the gross rent of a tract of land is $1000 a year, and it is subject to no taxes, the market value, assuming the usual rate of interest to be 5 per cent. will be $20,000. But if it is subject to an annual tax of $200, the net rent being thus reduced by 20 per cent. the price of the land will also be reduced by 20 per cent. to $16,000. If putting all the taxes upon rent would require a tax upon rent of $500 a year, this would only mean an addition of $300 to the tax; because the land was paying $200 already. But Mr. Mallock, Mr. Atkinson, and similar critics always assume that this change would involve the putting of an additional $500 on the rent, ignoring the fact that it already pays $200 of the amount.

§ 4. **Fundamental principles.** The principles governing these questions can be stated in a few brief propositions.

1. In economic science " rent " means only *ground*

rent, or the price which can be obtained for the use of the land alone, irrespective of improvements.

2. Ground rent, strictly speaking, is the amount paid by the tenant for the use of the land, without any deduction whatever, for taxes or anything else.

3. The market price or value of land, however, is always based upon an estimate of the probable *net* rent, deducting taxes.

4. The market value of a perpetual title to land is equal to the expected net annual rent (deducting taxes), multiplied by the number of years which, multiplied by the current rate of interest, would produce one hundred. Thus, if interest is five per cent., the title is worth twenty years' net rent.

5. The value of such a title, in economic science, is the same, only *not* deducting taxes.

6. The annual value or ground rent of land, in economic science, is on the average equal to the usual rate of interest upon the market value of its perpetual title, with the addition of all taxes annually levied exclusively upon that value.

The strictly scientific method of ascertaining the proportion of ground rent which would be taken by taxation if all taxes were concentrated upon it, would be to add the taxes now borne by rent to the present net rent, and then reckon the proportion of gross taxes to this gross rent. But as the writer made a calculation upon this principle some years ago, and it has apparently been too difficult for these critics to comprehend, a simpler method will now be adopted, more in accordance with the usages of real-estate dealers.

We will ascertain as nearly as possible:

1. The present net ground rent of a few important countries, states, and cities;

2. The entire burden of taxation in these places;

3. The amount of such taxation now borne by ground rent;

4. The amount of taxation which would be added to the present taxes on ground rent, if all taxes were collected from them, and which, therefore, is all that would be taken out of the net rents which land-owners now receive;

5. The proportion of net ground rent now collected by landlords, and remaining in their hands after paying existing taxes, which would be taken by this change in methods of taxation.

In these statistics, we shall take the liberty of generally omitting fractions of a thousand dollars or pounds, counting everything under five hundred as nothing, and everything above five hundred as one thousand. The results will be just as correct as if the usual wearisome details were given; and the figures will be vastly more intelligible.

§ 5. **Proportion of land values to real estate.** We shall adopt the uniform rule of estimating the value of the bare land at 60 per cent. of the value of all real estate. The substantial correctness of this estimate could be proved by an enormous mass of statistics. It is sufficient, however, to refer to the peculiarly careful and conscientious assessment of Boston, already quoted, as evidence of the fact in cities; while the analysis of the Massachusetts census, which will presently appear,[1] as well as the investigations of the Pennsylvania Tax Commission, give evidence of the fact in rural districts. The Pennsylvania return, it is true, reduces the average for the whole State to $51\frac{1}{2}$ per cent. But the returns from Philadelphia and other cities are plainly erroneous. They put the value of land in cities other than Pittsburgh at only 34 per

[1] Appendix to Chapter XII.

cent. of real estate.[1] But in Pittsburgh land is reported at 56 per cent. of real estate. Outside of cities, land is reported at about 70 per cent. of real estate. Correcting the error in cities, the average is about 60 per cent. A comparison of assessment returns from Boston, Buffalo, Cincinnati, Cleveland, Minneapolis, and many other cities, demonstrates that the 60 per cent. rule is, to say the least, fully as applicable to cities as it is to improved farms. Inquiry into British land values strongly indicates that they form 63 to 65 per cent. of all real-estate values there; but we may rest upon the minimum of 60 per cent., as being sufficiently near the truth to meet all cases.

It has been already shown that all the stationary property and franchises of railway, telegraph, gas, electric light, pipe line, steam heating, and similar companies are real estate, and that by far the greater part of the value in such concerns is a pure land value. These concerns will, therefore, be so treated, without further explanation. Much more than 60 per cent. of their incomes consists of pure ground rent; but they shall be put upon the same footing with all other real estate. With this allowance the tables hereafter given will err only upon the side of our opponents.

In adopting this general estimate of land values as 60 per cent. of all real estate, the estimate elsewhere of a much lower proportion of such values in farm lands is not forgotten. But that estimate refers only to cultivated farms, which constitute but a small part of the real estate

[1] This error is probably due to the very general division of land ownership, in Philadelphia and Eastern Pennsylvania cities, between pure ground rents and leaseholds. The value of a long lease is often very great; and this is part of economic land value or ground rent. The owner of a building, erected upon leased land, also owns the leasehold; and the usual rise in city land values often makes the leasehold alone worth one fourth to one third of the fee.

values of the United States, or of any state or country. Town lots alone far exceed in value all the farms of the United States; and among them the value of the land alone exceeds 60 per cent. of all real estate values. Uncultivated and unused lands form an enormous part of nominal farm values; and in their case, the pure land or ground-rent value is, of course, 100 per cent. of the whole. An estimate of 60 per cent. for the pure land value of all American real estate, taken together, is extremely moderate. For Great Britain, and still more for Ireland, it is far too low.

However, if any one doubts the correctness of this estimate, he can easily make a calculation, on the basis of those which follow, but reducing land values to 50 per cent. of real estate. He will find that it does not change the general result. Nothing short of a bold estimate of 30 per cent. as the proportion of land values, will suffice to refute the general conclusions here reached. Such an estimate would be absurd.

§ 6. **Rents in Great Britain and Ireland.** The theory of the insufficiency of Rent to meet Taxes having originated in England, it is as well to begin its refutation with that country, especially as its statistics of income are more full and correct than those of any other country. The returns for 1885 will be used, because they are the latest which have been used in this controversy or which have been made the basis of Mr. Giffen's valuable estimates of British wealth.

The whole amount raised by taxation, national and local, in Great Britain and Ireland for 1885 was £118,341,000.[1]

The official returns of the income tax, for 1885,[2] show

[1] *Statesman's Year Book*, 1888, p. 236.
[2] 28th *Report Internal Revenue Department.*

the following results. For the sake of brevity let us call these "British," instead of "British and Irish" incomes:

British Net Incomes from Real Estate; Returned in 1885.

I. From pure ground rents:

Manors, tithes, fines, etc......	£ 853,000	
Fishing and shooting rights....	572,000	
Market privileges and tolls....	607,000	2,032,000

II. From land and improvements:

Agricultural lands.............	£ 65,442,000
Houses and lots...............	127,050,000
Canals, water-works, mines, iron-works, gasworks, etc...	22,381,000
Railways.....................	33,050,000
	£247,923,000
60 % of this is.................................	£148,753,000
Net annual ground rents......................	£150,785,000

We must now consider the taxes which have been levied upon land, and which have therefore been deducted from the gross rent before these returns were made. They are as follows:

Land tax....................	£ 1,045,000	
Inhabited house duty.........	1,855,000	
Income tax on rents..........	3,605,000	
Local rates..................	37,846,000	
Tithes......................	4,054,000	£ 48,405,000

Sixty per cent. of this amount, being £29,043,000, must be deducted from the gross amount of taxes, because the landlords bear this already, and receive the £150,785,000 net.

Gross British taxes............	£118,341,000	
Deduct taxes now paid from ground rents..............	29,043,000	£ 89,298,000

This is the amount which would be collected from British rents, if all taxes were levied upon them. It is almost exactly 59 per cent. of British net ground rents, leaving all rent from houses and improvements untaxed. All British and Irish taxes could be paid out of existing rents and yet leave to the landlords a clear income of £61,487,000 ($300,000,000) per annum, *besides their house rents*, etc., amounting to at least as much more.

But this is a great understatement of the truth. It makes no account whatever of the constant rise in value of town lots. It assumes the absolute correctness of the returns of rent made by landlords. It assumes that the tax collectors have not lost sight of a single rent or failed to collect a single pound of what was due. It does not reckon the annual value of the palaces and parks of princes, dukes, earls, and other men of wealth, at any figure; because these places bring no actual income, and are not returned at all for income tax. The probability is that, if all such values could be ascertained, all the taxes of Great Britain would not absorb 45 per cent. of the present net value of the bare land.

§ 7. **Rents in the United States.** The census of 1890 estimates the total real "wealth" of the United States at $65,037,091,197; of which real estate is set down at $39,544,544,333.[1] But of this, real estate to the real value of $3,833,335,225 is exempt from taxation; and as there is no use in taxing public property, only to pay the tax out of the public treasury, exempt property may as well be excluded from these calculations.

The *assessed* valuation of property in 1890, which of course has little relation to the *real* value, was:

Real estate............	$18,956,556,675
Personal property.......	6,516,616,743
Total........	$25,473,173,418

[1] It has been denied that ground rents are real "wealth." But they are always so reckoned in statistics.

Thus it will be seen that real estate constituted 74½ per cent. of all assessed property, and therefore bore that share of *ad valorem* taxes. For convenience, this share may as well be called 75 per cent. The local *ad valorem* taxes amounted to $470,652,000. Reckoning land values as usual at 60 per cent of real estate, these values bore 60 per cent. of 75 per cent. of all local *ad valorem* taxes. This is exactly 45 per cent., leaving 55 per cent. to be borne by land improvements and personal property. Special taxes, such as licenses, succession taxes, corporation taxes, poll taxes, etc., are not included. But, as a large proportion of what is assessed as personal property is in fact real estate in a disguised form, the probability is that real estate actually bears more than 75 per cent. of all local taxes, of every description.

The valuation of real estate in the census was certainly not made upon any lower estimate of the rate of interest than 5 per cent. as even that would value land at twenty years' purchase. Only a small part of American real estate could be sold then or now at even that rate. Nevertheless, that rate is here accepted. It follows that rent must be reckoned at 5 per cent. on the capitalized value of land, since "land" in law is nothing but a name for a title to ground rents.

On this basis the following results are reached. They are extremely conservative; that is to say, they err on the side opposed to the argument here presented.

True Values of Real Estate, 1890.

Real estate, taxed as such[1]	$35,711,209,000
Railways	8,685,407,000
Mines and quarries	1,291,291,000
Telegraphs and canals, far more than	312,093,000
Total	$46,000,000,000
Land Values, 60 per cent. of this	$27,600,000,000

[1] Real estate worth over $3,800,000,000 is exempt from all taxation.

Ground Rental and Taxes in the U. S.

Rent, at 5 % on $27,600,000,000............		$1,380,000,000
National expenses...................	$357,889,000	
Local taxes	470,652,000	
	$828,541,000	
Deduct 45 % of local taxes, already laid on rent.......	211,793,000	
Taxation on present net rents, if all other taxes are repealed..................		616,147,000
Surplus rent.....................		$763,252,000

Thus all national and local taxes, if collected exclusively from ground rents, would absorb only 44½ per cent. of those rents, leaving to the owners of the bare land a clear annual rent of $763,252,000, *besides the absolutely untaxed income from all buildings and improvements upon their land.*

The above estimate of ground rents is very far below the reality. It does not include one dollar for the enormous value of oil wells, gas wells, pipe lines, the street privileges of gas, electric light, steam heating or water companies and other land privileges not expressly enumerated.

§ 8. **Rents in Pennsylvania.** Owing to a very remarkable example of public spirit, the State of Pennsylvania affords an opportunity for an inquiry of this kind, unequalled in any other State. A Revenue Commission has been formed by associations of private citizens, representing all interests, which has pursued a line of thorough investigation for several years past. Although its work is still incomplete and some of its statistics (as already pointed out) are plainly erroneous, they have been prepared in the best of faith and with unusual care; while their errors are easily found and readily corrected.

In round numbers the Commission estimates the entire

wealth of Pennsylvania, in 1892, at a true value of $9,692,000,000. Of this, $1,250,000,000 are reported as "moneyed capital." This is an obvious error, in a computation of real wealth. Moneyed capital cannot mean anything else than debts and credits. Whatever it adds at one end of the total wealth must be taken off at the other, as previously explained in this book. Deducting this item there remains real "wealth" (reckoning land values as part of wealth) to the amount of $8,500,000,000. On the basis of a full report of fire insurance in the State, the Commission estimates that $5,000,000,000 of this amount is of an insurable nature, that is, the value of buildings and chattels. This leaves the value of the bare land (which is the only thing incapable of being destroyed by insurable risks) at about $3,500,000,000, or a trifle more than 41 per cent. of the value of all wealth. Now this result, which is reached without any reference to the national census, and by a process utterly different from that which led to the conclusions given above, as to the United States at large, is nevertheless in perfect harmony with those conclusions. The estimated value of the land of the United States, given above, was 42 per cent. of all "wealth." The estimate of land values in Pennsylvania is over 41 per cent.

The entire local taxation of Pennsylvania in 1892 was $49,383,906. Of this there was levied upon real estate, in various forms, $36,000,000, as follows:

```
Taxes on "real estate"..................... $32,645,631
  "    " railways.........................    2,146,331
  "    " other land-owning corporations:
          about $1,200,000, say.............    1,208,038
                                              -----------
                                              $36,000,000
```

Sixty per cent. of this is $21,600,000; and this was the amount borne by the land values of Pennsylvania in 1892.

The proportion of federal taxation which would have fallen upon Pennsylvania, had federal taxes been direct, and levied in proportion to population, as required by the Constitution, was less than $30,000,000. But if levied in proportion to land values alone, it would be about $36,000,000. These figures furnish all materials necessary to determine the effect upon Pennsylvania land-owners of a concentration of taxes upon ground rents.

PENNSYLVANIA.

Ground Rents and Taxes of 1892.

Rent, at 5 % on $3,500,000,000............		$175,000,000
Federal taxes.........................	$36,000,000	
Local taxes...........................	49,384,000	
	$85,384,000	
Deduct 60 % of real-estate taxes, already paid	21,600,000	
Taxation on present net rents, if all other taxes are repealed.....................		63,784,000
Surplus rent....................		$111,216,000

Thus all national and local taxes, if collected only from ground rents, would absorb less than 36 per cent. of those rents in Pennsylvania, leaving to the land-owners a clear income of over $111,000,000 per annum, besides the untaxed income from their buildings and other improvements.

It will be noticed that a much smaller proportion of ground rent seems to be required for the payment of all taxes in Pennsylvania, than in the United States at large. This apparent discrepancy is due to the fact that the valuation of real estate, made by the Pennsylvania Commission, was 25 per cent. higher than the census valuation of 1890.

If the census estimates should be accepted with reference to Pennsylvania, as in other cases, the result would be as follows:

PENNSYLVANIA.

Ground Rents in 1890 : Taxes in 1892.

Land values, per census 1890, $2,810,000,000		
Rent at 5 %................................		$140,500,000
Federal taxes.............................	$36,000,000	
Local taxes...............................	49,384,000	
	$85,384,000	
Deduct taxes falling on ground rents in 1892	21,600,000	
Taxation on net rents of 1892, if all other taxes were repealed.....................		63,784,000
Surplus rent........................		$76,716,000

On the basis of the census estimates of value, therefore, the concentration of all taxes upon ground rents would absorb about 45½ per cent. of Pennsylvania net rents. This, it will be seen, is nearly the same proportion of rent which would appear, from the census, to be subject to absorption by such taxation, if applied to the United States as a whole.

§ 9. **Rents in Connecticut.** The State of Connecticut having been cited by some advocates of the personal property tax, as an example of the insufficiency of ground rents to support the whole burden of taxation, let us examine its record.

It appears, by the report of the Special Commission on Taxation, in 1887, that the local taxes of Connecticut then amounted to about $6,600,000, that the average tax rate was 1⅞ per cent., but railways were separately assessed and taxed exactly 1 per cent. The assessed value of real estate was $251,000,000; of which land values, at the usual rate of 60 per cent., would amount to $150,000,000. Railway property within the State was known to be worth, at regular market prices, $62,000,000 ; and it was assessed at its full value, the tax being made low on account of the known undervaluation of all other property. The land value in railways, at 60 per cent., amounted to $37,000,000.

The census of 1890 gives the following returns of the true market value of real estate in Connecticut.

CONNECTICUT.

True Values of Real Estate, 1890:

Real estate, returned as such....................	$543,421,891
Railways.......................................	54,550,504
Mines and quarries.............................	3,108,787
Canals, telegraphs, etc.[1]......................	14,753,310
	$615,834,492

Sixty per cent. of this for land values amounts to $369,500,000. We can now calculate

Connecticut Ground Rents, 1890 ; and Taxes, 1887.

Net ground rent, at 5 % on $369,500,000...................		$18,475,000
Federal taxes, apportioned on basis of rents	$4,800,000	
Local taxes.............................	6,600,000	
	$11,400,000	
Deduct taxes already laid on ordinary land values :		
$150,000,000 at 1⅞ %........ $2,812,500		
Do. on railways at 1%........ 370,000......	3,182,500	
Taxation on present net rents, if all other taxes are repealed..		8,217,500
Surplus rents...		$10,257,500

[1] This item includes shipping. But as gasworks and other immensely valuable franchises on land are not included, this item is not too large.

The concentration of all taxes upon the ground rents of Connecticut, therefore, would not absorb more than 44½ per cent. of those net rents, leaving to the land-owners a clear income of over $10,000,000 per annum, besides all their income from buildings and improvements.

§ 10. **Rents in Boston.** For the purposes of solving the problem submitted by Mr. Edward Atkinson, concerning the city of Boston, let us accept his figures, although they are not brought quite up to the date of 1890, and certainly understate the value of land.

His figures are given for 1888, and are as follows:

Land, assessed value...........................	$333,000,000
Buildings, " "	230,000,000
Personal property "	201,000,000

The whole amount of State and local taxes in Boston, in 1888, is given by Mr. Atkinson at $10,000,000 per annum; and he estimates the national taxes at "a sum as large, if not larger than all the State, county, city, and town taxes combined." But in this he is much mistaken. For many years local taxation has exceeded national taxation; and, as we have already shown, the State and local taxes assessed upon property by its value, *exclusive* of licenses, succession taxes and many others, exceeded, in 1890, the whole amount of national expenditures by about $113,000,000. In 1888 a direct tax of $300,000,000 would have amply sufficed to cover all the expenditures of the federal government, pensions included.

Apportioned according to population, as the Constitution requires, Boston's share of such a direct tax would have been $2,100,000.[1] Apportioned according to the value of land, either with or without improvements, Boston's share of such a direct tax would have been much

---

[1] Population, 1890: United States, 62,622,000; Boston, 446,000.

less than $4,500,000. The latter figure may be accepted, not only as affording stronger support to Mr. Atkinson's theory, but also as based upon just principles, in accordance with which it may be assumed that the Federal Constitution would be amended, whenever strictly direct taxation is adopted.

It may be assumed with entire certainty, in this case, as in others, that the assessors' estimate of the value of real estate was based upon the theory that it was renting for at least 5 per cent. per annum, net, on its capital value: for it is incredible that the assessors should have valued land at more than twenty times its annual rent. The annual rental value of the bare land of Boston in 1888 was therefore at least 5 per cent. on $333,000,000; that is to say, $16,650,000. The tax rate was $13.50 per $1000, or $4,500,000 on the bare land.

On this basis, and giving the benefit of every doubt in favor of Mr. Atkinson's views, the following conclusions are reached:

Boston Ground Rents and Taxes in 1888.

Ground rent, at 5 % of $333,000,000		$16,650,000
Federal taxes	$4,500,000	
Local taxes	10,000,000	
	14,500,000	
Deduct taxes on land values already paid	4,500,000	
Taxation on present net rents, if all other taxes are repealed		10,000,000
Surplus rent		$6,650,000

Thus all national and local taxes, if concentrated upon the ground rents actually found and assessed by the assessors of Boston, would absorb barely 60 per cent. of those rents, leaving to Boston land-owners a clear income of over $6,650,000 per annum, besides the untaxed income from buildings and other improvements.

§ 11. **Omissions from Boston rents.** Thus far it has been assumed that the figures of Boston assessors, upon which Mr. Atkinson relies, correctly represent the market value of all Boston land.

This concession has been made for the sake of argument; but it is utterly unjustifiable. No assessors in any city, however faithful in the performance of their duty, ever appraised land at its full market value, or anywhere near it. If the Boston assessors have appraised land at even 80 per cent. of its fair value, they have done their duty more faithfully than any other assessors in the United States. It may be said, however, that assessors never will do better, and therefore that in estimating the burden of taxation under the proposed system we must be content to value land on the basis of the best known assessments. The answer to this is, that we are not now seeking to know what will be the *apparent* burden of taxation upon ground rents, when this system goes into effect, but are inquiring what would be the real, *bona fide* burden thus imposed. And in order to judge of this we must calculate upon the basis of actual values, and not of mere assessed values.

But it is not necessary to enter into this question just now. Even accepting the official assessment, these figures show upon their face that the assessors have omitted from their estimate of land values in Boston some items of immense importance. Where is there any account made of the privileges conferred over and under Boston streets, upon railway, telegraph, telephone, gas, electric light, steam heating companies, etc.? So far as these corporations actually own, in their own names and of record, offices and buildings, over which they have exclusive control, like any other private land-owner, such property is assessed, but only at the same rate per square foot as other private land. But not one dollar of the value of the franchises of any of these corporations, or of the privileges which they have over and under Boston streets, is included in the assessors' estimate of land value. This will appear even more clearly upon examination of the assessors' annual reports. Such franchises and privileges are never assessed under the head of "land" in any State of the Union.

No doubt the Boston assessors and Mr. Atkinson were astonished at the suggestion, made some years ago, that all these franchises and privileges come within the definition of "land"; but they certainly do, both under the principles of economic science and under the plain terms of American law. They are "hereditaments,"[1] which form a part of "land," under both Massachusetts[2] and New York law[3]; although exempted from taxation by statute in New York, and by the "dead hand" of Chief Justice Shaw in Massachusetts.[4] Applying this principle to railroad, telegraph, gas, and other corporate privileges, in or over the streets of Boston, there can be no doubt that the land values appertaining to these franchises would be eagerly bid for at $3,000,000 per annum. The whole

[1] Smith v. New York, 68 N. Y., 552.
[2] *Rev. Stat.* ch. 3, § 7.
[3] 1 *Rev. Stat.*, 750.
[4] This famous judge, although undoubtedly honest, made some of the worst decisions in favor of corporations, which can be found in judicial history. He invented the theory under which masters are exempted from liability to servants for the negligence of co-servants. And he declared the roadbed of all railroads to be exempt from taxation, *because* the roads are permitted to acquire land under the power of "eminent domain" as for a public use (Worcester *v.* Western R. R. Co., 4 Metc., 564). The courts of New York, and probably of every other State, have treated this amazing doctrine as hardly worthy of discussion.

of this large sum is entirely omitted from the official estimate of ground rents in Boston; and, therefore, at twenty years' purchase, the land of Boston has been undervalued to the extent of $60,000,000.

This estimate is confirmed by the census of 1890, which shows that the real values of real estate, including these franchises, were nearly 30 per cent. higher than the assessed values in Massachusetts. The official figures for Boston alone are not at present accessible; but there is every reason for believing that the undervaluation there was as great at least as in the rest of the State, since Boston has more valuable franchises than any other part of the State. In view of these facts let us revise the foregoing table, on the basis of an addition of only 25 per cent. instead of 30.

Boston Ground Rents and Taxes, 1888.

Corrected by reference to Census.

Ground rent, assessed as such	$16,650,000	
Correction of under-assessment per census	4,162,000	$20,812,000
Federal taxes	$ 4,500,000	
Local taxes	10,000,000	
	$14,500,000	
Deduct taxes on land values already paid	4,500,000	
Taxation on present net rents, if all other taxes are repealed		10,000,000
Surplus rents		$10,812,000

The concentration of all taxation upon ground rents, in Boston, would not, therefore, absorb as much as 48 per cent. of those rents.

§ 12. Summary. All the foregoing calculations have been made without any preconceived theory as to the proportion which taxation would probably bear to rent, and without any anticipation that there would be much uniformity in the results obtained from such widely separated and widely different communities. Let us now compare these results, reckoning the British pound at $4.85.

	Net Ground Rent Less Present Tax.	Additional Tax.	Proportion Taken by Tax.
Great Britain	$ 731,307,000	$433,095,000	59 %
United States	1,380,000,000	616,748,000	44¼ %
Pennsylvania	140,500,000	63,784,000	45¼ %
Connecticut	18,475,000	8,217,000	44½ %
Boston	20,812,000	10,000,000	48 %

The uniformity of result, where the figures are based upon the same census, as in the United States at large, Pennsylvania, and Connecticut, is remarkable.

In Great Britain the estimate of ground rent does not allow a dollar for the value of vacant land or unoccupied houses, parks or pleasure grounds. The magnificent estate of Chatsworth is rated at only $3000 per annum. An addition of one third to the values included above would be far below the truth. With such an addition, the proportion of taxes to British rents would be reduced below 44½ per cent.

All attainable statistics thus point to the conclusion that the entire cost of the most expensive and even extravagant governments in civilized countries could be placed upon ground rents, without taking in taxation even half of the present net income of land-owners from that source alone.

The land-owning reader may be impatient and indignant with this cold statement of a result which, as he will think, means ruin to him. But he must remember that this chapter is devoted to the single inquiry: "Is Rent enough to meet Taxes?" leaving other questions for future consideration. In a later part of this book, those other questions will be fairly met and dealt with.

Anticipating, however, for a moment, one of those important questions, let it be observed that no allowance has been made, in the foregoing figures, for the undeniable fact that the land-owning class own not merely the land but also all the buildings and improvements upon land, besides a vastly larger share of personal property than any other class of the cummunity. Under the present system, *all* these things are taxed. Under a system of natural taxation, *none* of them would be taxed, except the value of the land alone. It will presently be shown that the benefits conferred upon nine tenths of the land-owning class, by the release of all their other property, earnings and expenses from taxation, would be enormous. But that does not find its proper place in this chapter, which has to do with no other inquiry than the sufficiency of ground rents to supply government revenue.

§ 13. **Ground rents in rural districts.** Having analyzed the cases of large cities and large states, fully settled and highly civilized, and found that a moderate tax on their ground rent is sufficient for all their needs, there remain for consideration villages, small towns, and half settled states or territories on the border of civilization.

It is said, with great confidence, that the land of these communities is of no value, and therefore that a tax upon this no-value land could not support government in these districts. Of course, if the assertion is true the argument is conclusive. But the assertion is not true; and the argument would apply only to a very limited district, even if it were based upon truth.

No one lives permanently, within the real dominion of any government, on land which has no value. Robinson

Crusoe, living alone, occupied land which was of great utility to him; although it could not produce economic "value" (that is, value in exchange) until some one else came upon the island. But, until then, he had no government. When Friday landed, Robinson formed a government of one; and economic rent or land value began. The price which Friday was glad to pay, for permission to live on the island, was his rent; and that rent was, as we all know, amply sufficient to defray all the expenses of government. Wherever any government exists it necessarily, in the very nature of things, assumes the ownership of all land within its limits; and ground rent at once begins. Between the government and the citizen any land, however poor, has a market value. The citizen who inflexibly insists that it has not is invited to emigrate, and is forced to give place to some one who has a different opinion.

Although it is ideally conceivable that a state of things might exist in which land might have no exchangeable value, as between private individuals, no one has ever known that state of things to exist, where even a hundred people live in civilized community together; and such a state of things, as between any government and any person receiving any benefit from that government upon land permanently appropriated by him, is inconceivable.

§ 14. **Ground rents always exceed cost of government.** Nor can the average annual cost of necessary government for any community ever be greater than the average annual value of its land. To say that it can, is a contradiction in terms. How can any government be *necessary*, which costs more than the privilege of living under it is worth? And what is the cost of the privilege of living in any particular place, except the ground rent of that place? It makes no difference how you assess the price of the privilege. A landlord can, if he chooses, fix his asking price for rent upon a computation of his tenant's personal property. If the price thus fixed is less than the market value of the land, the tenant will gladly pay it, and bless the stars which gave him a fool for a landlord. If it is more, the tenant will move away, and the landlord will get nothing. The state can do no more. No one will pay more taxes than the privilege of residing within the jurisdiction of the state is worth. If any one pays less, he is better off than people who live in another place and pay full value. This difference is so much natural rent; which he puts into his own pocket or is compelled to pay to a private landlord.

Ground rent, therefore, is invariably sufficient to meet all the expenses of necessary government. But as government never exists where society does not exist, and as society offers many advantages in addition to the mere benefits of government, the privilege of living in society is worth much more than the mere cost of government. This privilege is dependent upon the privilege of living within a tract of land in which society exists. Outside of such land, there is other land, with no society and no government. The difference between the value or no-value of the right to live in solitude and the value of the right to live in society is so much economic rent.

Rent, therefore, will at all times, in all places and in all circumstances, exceed the entire cost of necessary government.

§ 15. **Proper distribution of government cost.** But a great central government finds it for the advantage of the whole nation to maintain much more complex and expensive government in places like Alaska, Wyoming, and Arizona, than is really needed for the small number of people actually residing there. It therefore maintains territorial governments, at the expense of the more advanced States; not because Arizona needs so much government, but because New York, Chicago, and St. Louis need to have new countries developed faster than the residents of those territories need for their own benefit.

So great cities need costly roads through little villages, which would otherwise be satisfied with mule tracks. Roads ought to be a State charge; and it is now seen that the failure to treat them as such has been a disastrous mistake. The consequence of leaving roads to be managed by local authorities has been that not one road in a hundred, throughout the United States, is properly laid out or respectably maintained. The governor of Pennsylvania, several years ago, called attention to this notorious fact and suggested that roads ought to be taken under the control of the State. This example has been followed by the governors of New York, New Jersey, and other States.

The administration of justice should not be left to the control or the charge of small towns. Court houses and jails ought to be, at the very least, a county charge, if not furnished at the expense and under the supervision of the State. The State cannot afford to tolerate injustice within the limits of any township; and while it may be that all these matters can be judiciously left to the control of large districts, like a county, it is not desirable that they should be intrusted to the control of each little township for itself. Consequently, the expense of court houses and jails should be provided and their management should be controlled by counties, if not by the whole State. The State of New York is properly taking all lunatic asylums under its own charge.

For similar reasons schools should be maintained at the expense and under the control of large districts. It is no more for the interest of the State of New York to permit ignorance to prevail in the woods of Hamilton and Ulster, than it is for the interest of the United States to allow robbery to flourish unchecked in Arizona. This is not a mere question of financial ability. There are many townships which have abundant means to provide for the proper education of their children, which, nevertheless, have but little interest in seeing the work done, and the residents of which are in fact so isolated from the rest of the world that they have no idea how such work should be done. This principle is partially recognized in New York. Public schools are supported by State appropriations; although they are not controlled by the State as fully as they should be.

The expenses of government will in the future more and more tend to centralization in counties, if not in States. Of course it will never do for the State to pay the bills, where it does not control the outlay. Whatever roads, courts, jails, or schools are paid for by the State should be controlled by the State; otherwise townships which would receive all the benefit of expenditure would feel no direct interest in diminishing its burden.

§ 16. **Rent sufficient, when burdens just.** Now, no one seriously maintains that the ground rent of any county in the thickly settled parts of the United States is not amply sufficient to defray all the expenses of government properly chargeable to that county, exclusive of federal taxes; and no one can successfully claim that any State east of the Mississippi River is so poor that its ground rent would not suffice to defray all its own government expenses, as well as the proportion of federal taxation which would fall upon it under the existing Federal Constitution, which apportions such taxes according to population, instead of according to wealth. It may be claimed that some of the very new and thinly settled States could not bear the burden of federal taxation on that basis, in addition to their own expenses, without trenching upon something besides ground rent ; although, for the reasons above stated, even this is highly improbable. It is quite certain that when taxation is adjusted, as it must finally be, in proportion to the ground rent of every State and county, the cost of government will not exceed, nor even equal, the amount of such rent in any county of the United States. When the burden of maintaining government is apportioned, as it also must be, between States, counties, cities, townships, and villages, in such manner as to relieve the smaller divisions from burdens which do not properly belong to them, there will no longer be any question in the mind of any reasonable man as to the sufficiency of ground rent, in every corner of the United States, to bear all the expenses of government, and yet to leave a generous margin.[1]

[1] The statements in the text can be illustrated by reference to the appropriations for town purposes, made by several farming towns of small population in Massachusetts in the spring of 1895. With each town is given the population in 1890, number of acres assessed, and appropriations, including highways, paupers, etc., and schools.

Berkshire County.

Town.	Acres.	Population.	Highways.	Schools.	Paupers, etc.	Total Appropriations.
Alford	7,172	297	$ 400	$ 600		$1,075
Egremont	11,107	845	1,000	1,000		3,060
Hinsdale	13,745	1,739	1,800	4,025	$1,100	9,840
Lanesboro'	17,332	1,018	1,190	1,700	1,000	7,020
Savoy	19,917	569	1,000	700		2,500
Tyringham	10,845	412	800	950		2,715
Richmond	11,321	796	1,500	2,050	700	5,725
Clarksburg	7,749	884	1,000	1,500		3,000

Hampden County.

Town.	Acres.	Population.	Highways.	Schools.	Paupers, etc.	Total Appropriations.
Chester	21,588	1,295	2,400	2,000	1,400	9,339
Hampden	11,752	831	750	1,825	600	3,960
Holland	7,120	201	400	200	100	1,050
Montgomery	8,586	266	700	600	200	1,915

Hampshire County.

Town.	Acres.	Population.	Highways.	Schools.	Paupers, etc.	Total Appropriations.
Westhampton	15,282	477	1,000	1,150	500	3,100
Total		9,660	$13,940	$18,300	$5,600	$54,299

These statistics are taken from the Springfield *Republican*. They all tell

To state the case again in another form, the whole matter can be summed up by saying that it is impossible that any government can be *necessary*, which costs more than the ground rent of the district which is called upon to pay for it ; since that rent will always represent, to the fullest extent, not only all that such government is reasonably worth to the inhabitants of that district, but also the full market value of all other advantages which they derive from human society, as it actually exists among them. Any pretended taxation which takes more from the people than this is extortion, not genuine taxation.

the same story. Highways (including bridges), schools, and paupers account for two thirds to three fourths of all local expenses in these little townships.

Taken altogether, highways cost 26%, schools 34%, and paupers 10% of all town expenses; making 70% of the whole expended for purposes which ought to be provided for by State taxation, and kept under State control. In New York schools and paupers are already provided for by a general tax, and highways soon will be.

Observe the large area and small population of most of these towns, especially Alford, Savoy, Tyringham, Holland, Montgomery, and Westhampton, which are devoted almost exclusively to farming, and where there are 130 to 190 acres for each family. Is it reasonable to cast the whole expense of highways through this large territory on such a sparse population? Can we wonder that country roads are bad?

Of course a State tax would be levied on these towns, as well as upon others. But they would pay only according to the proportion which the value of their ground rents bore to those of the entire State. Their gross taxes would be reduced by at least 50 per cent.

That this result would follow, is conclusively shown by the experience of New York. While all counties are taxed, for State purposes, in proportion to the value of their real estate alone, the State repays to every one of the farming counties (being 40 out of the entire 60), *for school purposes alone*, more than the whole county contribution to the State tax. And, in addition, the State provides for all their paupers and insane free of county charge.

The adoption of a natural and rational system of local taxation, combined with a proper distribution of expenses, would thus relieve the farming population in Massachusetts from one half of their present burdens. It may be safely assumed that it would have the same effect in other commercial or manufacturing States.

CHAPTER XI.

JUSTICE OF NATURAL TAXATION.

§ 1. **A tax on taxation only.** If the proposed method of taxation is not just, it is not natural. But if it is natural, it is just.
To state the case is to demonstrate the justice of the tax. For what is here proposed is simply this:
To tax the proceeds of taxation, and nothing else.
For ground rent *is* taxation, and nothing else. The power to collect ground rent is a delegated power of taxation. Can anything be more just than for the State to draw its revenue from the proceeds of such taxation and from nothing else?

§ 2. **Privilege of collection implies duty of payment.** The duty of providing for the whole support of government is indissolubly attached to the right of collecting ground rent. The landlord, as the only natural tax-gatherer, is also the only natural revenue-provider. Every man who buys the privilege of taxation assumes, by the very act, a proportionate share of the burden of government expenses. No lapse of time, no misconception of the situation, no unwise or excessive payment for the privilege can ever relieve him from this inherent obligation. The State may justly resume its rights, to this extent, at any moment, even if it has left them in abeyance for ages. It ought not to demand compensation for the past; because in the United States, at least, the past misappropriation of these taxes has taken place under the eyes and with the free consent of the people. But nothing has happened which deprives the State of a perfect right to demand performance of this duty for the future.

The case would be entirely clear to every disinterested mind, if a simple power of levying taxation had in terms been granted to a private citizen. Thus, if the State of New York had granted to the first Astor and his heirs forever the right to exact an annual poll tax of one dollar per head from all inhabitants of the State, either without consideration or for a cash payment of one dollar for each inhabitant then living, nobody outside of the Astor family would hesitate about the matter. Much less, if the State had granted to the Astors the exclusive right to collect for their own use all the taxes which should ever be levied in any form whatever, would there be any doubt that the State would have both the legal and moral right to require the Astors to pay, out of the proceeds, all the necessary expenses of government. No judge would hesitate a moment to say that such a condition was implied in the original grant, notwithstanding any words to the contrary; or else he would hold the grant utterly void, as beyond the power of any legislature.

Yet this is exactly a parallel case. Nay, it is not too much to say that it is the very case in question. The State, in parcelling out the land within its borders among private owners, gave to them the whole power of taxation which, in the nature of things, could exist at the foundation of any State. For in any newly settled country there is absolutely nothing to tax, except the rental value of the land.

§ 3. **Illustrations from American history.** Of this fact, there have been repeated illustrations in the recent history of the United States. Within the memory of most living electors, Kansas, Nebraska, North Dakota, South Dakota, Colorado, Wyoming, Idaho, and Oklahoma have been opened for the first time to settlement. Prior to that time it was not lawful for any white man to take up a permanent residence within their limits; they had no local government and no taxes.

When such a territory was opened, its first need was some government. This was, as a matter of fact, provided by the United States, which were only partly reimbursed by taxation. But if this had not been done, what would have been the natural course of events? The people would have organized a provisional government, as they actually did in California in 1849. There were no houses, no barns, no improvements, no mortgages, no personal property fixed long enough in any one spot to be capable of assessment. What was there which could possibly have been taxed in the first week of territorial existence? Nothing, except the value of the land. Was that sufficient? Let the experience of Oklahoma answer. Scores of thousands of people swarmed to the border, kept out by government rifles until the hour struck at which they were allowed to enter. Then they rushed in at full speed, tearing their way like mad bulls—where? To the land offices; where they could purchase for a trifling sum the legal right to tax those who fell behind in the race. What was there then to tax? Nothing but the privilege of living on the best tracts of land. Not the farming districts, but the town lots were the prizes in view. These were what the federal officials seized for themselves. These were the rewards which tempted men to perjury and fraud, as well as to zeal and long self-denial.

And what did the government find to tax at that moment? No houses; no chattels; nothing but the privilege of settling upon the land; and from this it derived an immediate and large revenue; although it threw away nine tenths of what it might have received, to be scrambled for by the owners of fast horses and by its own knavish servants, leaving the honest mass of settlers to pay tribute to the favored few, who swore that they meant to settle on the land, and knew that they were swearing to a lie. All the powers of local government were then turned over to the few thousand voters, who thus gained possesssion of the land, either direct from the federal government, for nothing, or from those who had forestalled them by speed or fraud, for a price. Still there was practically nothing to tax, except land values. The annual ground rents were amply sufficient to pay all the cost of government. But in the course of a year or two, other settlers drifted in. The landowners, being still in the majority, not only exacted in rent from the newcomers the full market value of the privilege of living in the territory, but further proceeded to shift as much of the burden of taxation from their own shoulders as they possibly could, by taxing personal property.

Now is this the natural and sensible method of opening new territory? Is there not a better way? Would not common sense and science agree that the true policy of the nation would have been to say to all the proposing settlers: "Take this land. Charge what you please to new settlers, who wish to buy of you the privilege of living there. But out of the sums thus collected you must pay all the expenses of government, local and national. You shall not make your tenants pay the cost of government, in addition to the rent which they pay you for the mere privilege of living on the land which has been given you free of charge." Clearly, if there is anything unfair in such an arrangement, it is not unfair to the gratuitous grantees of the land.

§ 4. "**Confiscation.**" It will be said, of course, that this method of taxation is mere "confiscation"; and, to the minds of many, this will be a conclusive objection. It is to be regretted that the brilliant author of *Progress and Poverty* should have even once used this word; thus seeming to identify the cause of equal taxation with apparent robbery and to confound justice with injustice. Although such may not have been its original meaning, yet by long usage "confiscation" is understood to mean a punishment for crime or moral incapacity. We are not at liberty to confiscate, in this sense, either land or its rent.

But no question of confiscation arises in the case. If all the land belongs to all the people, if past generations had no power to alienate it from the control of the present, if its rent is now wrongfully withheld from the people, their taking the whole of it would be merely a just resumption of their own, not confiscation. And this is all which Henry George ever meant; as page after page of his book clearly shows. It is not necessary, however, to discuss that question here. We are not inquiring into the wrongs of the past or even into the general rights of the people in the present. We are considering only the proper method of raising *necessary* revenue.

§ 5. "**Class legislation.**" The only pretence for charging that this method is a measure of confiscation is founded upon the allegation that it is unjust to put the whole burden of taxation upon a single class. In the light of past history, during which the owners of land have used all their powers, with immense success, to get rid of all taxes upon themselves and to cast the whole burden upon the landless poor, their present remonstrances, sometimes pathetic, sometimes ferocious, against a reversal of their methods, are highly entertaining.

Every tariff duty, every excise tax, every indirect tax bears witness to the persistent ingenuity with which the collectors of rent, the natural tax, have shifted the burdens of public taxation upon other shoulders. Not one dollar of our vast federal revenue is collected from rent. Nine tenths of it is collected from the comparatively poor. Great Britain has been hitherto governed by large landlords: America by small ones. Both alike have evaded the taxation of rent as much as possible. Both alike have never hesitated to ruin vast numbers of their fellow citizens, by sudden, arbitrary and disastrous changes in methods of taxation. Both alike have never dreamed of allowing the smallest compensation to the victims of their caprice. But, as only great landlords can make a profit out of such methods, British landlords have made themselves wealthy in this way; while the mass of American land-owners have plundered themselves for the benefit of a few.

§ 6. **Compensation.** There is no precedent for the doctrine that taxation must be spread over the whole community, and still less for the novel claim that the State is bound to compensate taxpayers for the payment of taxes. When will any congress compensate Americans whose property was destroyed by changes in the tariff?

Originally, all land was granted by the State upon the express or clearly implied condition that the grantee should provide for all the expenses of government. The land-owners gradually shifted the burden off their own shoulders, by new taxes on the non-voting population. But even they had not the audacity to make a perpetual covenant between themselves and the government which they controlled, for exemption from taxation. The plea of their successors is that, by long failure on the part of the people to demand their rights and the performance of the conditions upon which the land was granted, landlords have been led to believe that such a demand would never be made; that many of them have paid large prices for the privilege of charging rent, in the belief that rent would never be taxed; and that it is unjust for the State to change its policy in this respect, without giving to them as much with one hand as it takes from them with the other.

The argument is just as valid in favor of kings and nobles; and it has been urged upon their behalf with equal sincerity. Down to 1788 French nobles were exempt from most taxes. Many men (like Beaumarchais) bought a title, partly for the sake of this exemption. The French Revolution swept away all these privileges, without a shred of compensation; and all the world now says that this was perfectly right. But to an army of tax-eaters in those days it seemed monstrously wrong. The parallel is complete.

§ 7. **Compensation for vested rights.** The concentration of all taxes upon ground rents, if enacted at the foundation of a state, would obviously be simple justice. Why is it not equally just at any later period? "Because," it is said, "there have been many changes of ownership: vested rights have sprung up: new men have bought the land from the original owners, paying a much larger price than they would have paid if it had been understood that rent would be taxed. Heavy taxation will destroy the market value of the land; and this would be robbery under the forms of law."

What is this land value, which is so sacred that it must not be heavily taxed? Nothing in the world except the value of a power, conferred upon individuals, to tax other individuals for the privilege of standing upon the earth. It is the only kind of property which cost the original owner nothing, in either wealth or labor. Every other form of property was called into being by honest human skill and labor, and was therefore fully paid for. Property in ground rents was, in every instance, originally acquired either by undertaking to bear the cost of government, as in feudal times, or by gift or theft, just as we have seen it acquired in Oklahoma. No doubt, thousands sacrificed much, in the pursuit of Oklahoma land, by hanging on the borders of the territory for weeks, waiting for the day upon which the gift was to be made. But by doing so they no more gave value for the land, than beggars give value for what they get, by standing hat in hand all day long.

It is true that this power to levy taxes upon other men has been sold, over and over again, at increasing prices, and is now generally held by men who paid something of value for it. But what of that? The State never pledged itself to exempt this privilege from taxation, or to limit the amount to which it will be taken for public purposes; and no legislature has any moral right to do so. The present owners of the taxing power have bought upon a speculation, and must take all the chances of speculation. Among those chances is the possibility that the State may call for no part of the tax collected under the name of rent, and, on the other hand, the possibility that it may call for nearly the whole of it. All other forms of property are bought on a similar speculation.

Iron, steel, glass, crockery, tin plates, buttons, laces, whisky, apples, eggs, horses, cattle, mortgage bonds, bank stocks, railway shares, and hundreds of other things are bought and sold, with full knowledge that there may be sudden and vast changes in the rates of taxation upon them, made without notice, without the slightest scruple, and without even a thought of compensation to the many who suffer thereby. The tax on whisky was suddenly raised to 50 cents, then to $1, then to $2, then reduced to 50 cents, then raised again to 90, and all without the slightest compensation to anybody. The tariff taxes were suddenly increased 50 per cent. all around, in 1864, in one night, without notice and without a dream of compensation.

Why, then, this amazing and unexampled tenderness for speculators in the privilege of taxing their fellow men? The answer is easy. Most of the losses arising from increase in other forms of taxation fall upon the masses of comparatively poor; because the burden of such taxes is shifted upon them. None of the loss arising from an increase of taxation upon ground rents would fall upon the poor; because that burden cannot be shifted upon anybody. It is the old, old story. The right of the rich to plunder the poor is a vested right, sacred, even in the eyes of the poor themselves, through long training in abject servility.

CHAPTER XII.

WHERE THE BURDEN FALLS.

§ 1. **Incidence of taxation.** No matter how necessary or beneficial it may be, taxation must always cast a burden upon some one. No matter how justly this burden may be distributed, it still falls somewhere; and it is necessary that we should know where it falls. The great change from unnatural and unjust taxation to natural and just taxation cannot be made without increasing the burdens of *some* classes; and every class will properly insist upon knowing how its interests will be affected. Let us therefore now inquire upon what classes the burden will be increased, and upon what classes it will be diminished. Or, in technical language, what will be the "incidence" of natural taxation?

It must never be forgotten, however, that the burdens of natural and of unnatural taxation are not the same. It has long ago been explained that the burdens imposed by the clumsy and corrupting methods of taxation, now in force, are twice or thrice as heavy as would be the necessary burdens of a natural system. But, as readers are sure to forget this, their attention will be recalled to it more fully at a later stage, when some results will appear which, for want of bearing this in mind, will seem at first incredible.

In the United States, the three principal classes for consideration are wage-earners, farmers, and other landowners. To some extent these different classes mingle together. But only a small minority of farmers work for wages (for of course farm laborers are not included under the head of farmers); and a vast majority of wage-earners own either no land or so little as to have no effect upon their interest in this question.

A division of the people into these classes, however, would be very incomplete. There is a considerable number of persons who do not work for mere daily wages or on farms and who own no land. The correct division would be into two classes, the land-owning and the landless. But American traditions so closely identify farmers with land-owners that farmers, whether owning or hiring farms, must be set apart as a class by themselves, in any popular discussion of these subjects. The most convenient arrangement, therefore, for practical purposes, seems to be to consider the interests of the people in three classes, not scientifically distinct, as follows:

1. The landless class.
2. The land-owners.
3. The farmers, whether owning or hiring land.

§ 2. **Relative numbers of different classes.** The relative proportions of these classes were ascertained, for the first time, by the census of 1890.

The whole number of families was........................12,690,152
Families on farms................. 4,767,179
Other families................................7,922,973   12,690,152

Families owning land.......................6,066,417
Families owning none.....................6,623,735   12,690,152

Owners of unincumbered land................4,369,527
Owners of incumbered land..................1,696,890
Owners of no land......................... 6,623,735   12,690,152

Families owning land, free and clear...........4,369,527
Families hiring or mortgaged................8,320,625   12,690,152

Male owners...................5,019,659
Female owners............ ...1,046,758   6,066,417

Male tenants........ 5,837,590
Female tenants....... 786,145   6,623,735   12,690,152

It is interesting to note the relative proportions in rural and urban districts. The census gives the figures separately for farms, for towns of 8,000 to 100,000 inhabitants, and for cities of over 100,000. From these figures an approximately correct table may be framed, under the heads of farms, villages, large towns, and cities, as follows:

	Land-owners.	Landless.	Total.
Farms............	3,142,746	1,624,433	4,767,179
Villages.........	1,849,700	2,374,860	4,224,560
Towns...........	629,092	1,120,487	1,749,579
Cities....	444,879	1,503,955	1,948,834
Total........	6,066,417	6,623,735	12,690,152

The number of adult male persons in the United States, in 1890, was returned at 16,940,311.

The numbers "engaged in gainful occupations"—in other words, earning their own living—was returned at 22,736,229; of whom 19,321,700 were over 20 years of age.

These figures show that more than half the heads of families, more than two thirds of the adult males, and over 70 per cent. of the persons earning their own living, belonged, in 1890, to the landless class.

As practically all adult males are possible voters, it thus appears that more than two thirds of the voters are landless.

Confining our views to the white voters, it appears that the number of white adult males was 15,199,856, while the number of white males owning the homes or farms in which they lived was 4,800,799. The landless whites, therefore, compose two thirds of the white voters.

The possible colored voters numbered 1,740,455. Of these only 218,860 owned homes or farms, being almost exactly one eighth of the whole, and leaving seven eighths in the landless class.

§ 3. **The landless.** The immense advantage which would be gained by the landless class, through the abolition of all taxes, except upon ground rents, is of course obvious. It would relieve them from all the taxes which they now pay, together with all the burdens, incidentally resulting from the present methods of taxation, which now fall upon them. They would continue to pay rent; but, while they now pay *both* rent and taxes, they would then pay rent alone.

Nine tenths of the absolutely landless persons belong to what is, for want of a better name, usually called the laboring class. The abolition of all indirect taxation, it has already been shown, would increase the possible savings of this class, fivefold (*Ante*, pp. 36, 37). Nothing need be added to what has been said on that subject.

The landless class, as will be seen by reference to the figures last given, constitutes more than half of the families and more than two thirds of the self-supporting population. It includes a majority of the voters, even upon farms, two thirds of the voters in villages, three fourths of the voters in large towns, and nearly, if not quite, seven eighths of the voters in cities.

§ 4. **The land-owners.** It has already been shown that the concentration of all American taxes upon American land-owners would not absorb half of their ground rents. But it would be a great mistake to assume that such taxation would absorb half of their whole income, or anything approaching to it. No allowance has thus far been made for the important fact that, considered as an entire class, *the owners of ground rents also own all the buildings and other improvements upon their land*, besides a much larger share of all personal property, in proportion to their number, than any other class of the community. All these things would be relieved from taxation under the system here proposed. *All* taxes on real estate and probably 75 per. cent. of the taxes on personal property are paid by land-owners.[1] They also pay at least their full share, in proportion to their numbers, of tariff and excise taxes, and of the burdens which indirectly flow from those taxes. As American land-owners constituted 48 per cent. of the heads of families in 1890, they will be released from 48 per cent. of those burdens, the amount of which was estimated, on a previous page, at $1,050,000,000 per annum.

The local taxes on both real and personal property in 1890 amounted to $470,652,000. As real property constituted three fourths of all assessed values, its owners paid three fourths of these taxes ($352,989,000), three fourths of the taxes on personal property ($88,248,000), and 48 per cent. of the $1,050,000,000 burden, created by federal indirect taxation ($504,000,000). These were the burdens borne by real-estate owners, *as a class*, in 1890: all of which would, under the taxation of ground rents alone, be replaced by a single tax of $828,541,000.

The effect of such a change in taxation, upon American owners of real estate, *taken as an entire class*, would be as follows:

American real-estate owners paid, in 1890, under the present system of taxation:

All local taxes on real estate..............	$352,989,000	
75 per cent. of local taxes on personal estate.	88,248,000	
48 per cent. of federal taxes and burdens attendant thereon......................	504,000,000	$945,237,000
They would pay, if all taxes were concentrated on ground rents:		
All local taxes.........................	$470,652,000	
All federal taxes.......................	357,889,000	828,541,000
Net *reduction* of burdens on real estate..............		$116,696,000

[1] Not more than one tenth of the persons who are not assessed for some land are ever assessed for any personal property, taking the whole country together.

§ 5. **An apparent impossibility explained.** This conclusion will, at first sight, seem impossible and perhaps. absurd. " What ! " the incredulous reader will exclaim; " do you expect us to believe that the concentration of all taxes upon real estate, whether including improvements or not, can possibly *reduce* the burdens of real estate owners ? The very idea is repugnant to common sense."

Nevertheless, the idea is well within the range of common sense. The hasty reader has forgotten that indirect taxes always involve enormous burdens in their train, not known as taxes, not collected for public use, not capable of accurate computation, but none the less real and heavy. These incidental burdens have been estimated, throughout this book, at $700,000,000 per annum. They include a large private profit, through enhanced prices, maintained by tariffs and excise laws ; and they also include a sum, quite as large, absolutely wasted, by keeping up prices on goods which, after all, do not afford an average profit to domestic producers. Land-owners *as* land-owners do not get the profit, and nobody gains by the waste.

No doubt a small section of the land-owning class do get a large share of the profits arising from the monopolies fostered by protective tariffs and excise taxes. But more than nine tenths of the land-owners derive no benefit from these monopolies. All of them must pay their proportion of the taxes and private tribute, levied by laws creating monopolies ; but the profit accruing goes to those who can run the monopolies, whether they own or only hire land.

Direct taxation would put an end to all such monopolistic profits and all the indirect effects of indirect taxation. Owners of land, who did not hold any share in tariff-bred or similar monopolies, would save, by substituting direct for indirect taxation, their share of the $700,000,000 annually lost to the people at large in this way. And this saving more than outweighs all the additional taxation falling upon them, through the exemption of labor and personal property from taxes.

Another reason is of even greater importance, and clears up the whole apparent mystery. These statistics show that, if all the land were owned by a class, on perfectly equal terms, in equal shares, they would *all* gain by direct taxation. But they do *not* stand on an equal footing or own equal shares. On the contrary, it is now undisputed that more than 75 per cent. in value of all American real estate, including railways, is owned by less than 10 per cent. of the whole number of land-owners. Indeed, it is practically undisputed that this amount is held by less than 5 per cent. of the whole number, and that half of all the value is held by one-hundredth of all owners.

This fact immediately puts a new light upon the whole question. Accepting the far too conservative estimate that one tenth of all the owners, or 600,000 families, own three fourths of all the land, and constructing a table, showing the effect of the change in taxation upon them, we should reach very different results.

These families, being much richer than the remaining 5,500,000, of course pay even now a much larger share of taxes of all kinds. Owning three fourths of all real estate, they must now pay three fourths of the taxes on that, or, in round numbers, $264,000,000. They doubtless pay one fourth of all personal taxes, or $29,000,000. Their quota of federal taxes, etc., would be very much larger than that of the same number of small land-owners. It would not be less than $200,000,000. On the other hand, this class includes nearly all those persons who derive profit from tariffs, monopolies, and bounties; all of which would be swept away by a natural system of taxation. This class, as a whole, would suffer some loss.

§ 6. **Where the burden would fall.** But the line must be drawn still higher up. The profits of artificial monopolies and bounties are almost entirely divided among less than 50,000 land-owners. The remaining 6,000,000 get practically none of these profits. The line of division, therefore, must be drawn between the 50,000 families, which own at least 30 per cent. of all the land values of the United States, and the 6,000,000, who own the remainder.

Allowing one half the burdens, indirectly resulting from tariffs and excise laws, to be mere waste, bringing no profit to anybody, still, in years of average prosperity, annual profits to the amount of $350,000,000 would remain ; of which more than $300,000,000 go to the 50,000 largest land-owners.

Let us now construct a table, showing the incidence of direct taxation upon

The 50,000 largest land-owners.

They paid, in 1890 :
30% of taxes on real estate..........	$106,000,000	
10% of " " personal estate.....	11,700,000	
10% of tariff, etc., taxes, profits, and waste.......................	105,000,000	$222,700,000
They gained profits from the tariff, etc..............		300,000,000
Their net profits from the system of indirect taxation were.........		77,300,000
Under direct taxation, they would make no tariff profits, and would pay 30% of all taxes.........		249,000,000
Their net *loss*, from direct taxation.................		$326,300,000

This explanation makes it easy to understand how the vast majority of land-owners may actually gain by assuming the whole burden of direct taxation. By so doing, they get rid of paying a tribute of $350,000,000 to a small band of bounty-fed capitalists, and of an annual waste of $350,000,000 more. The loss of this tribute will fall entirely upon the few who depend upon unjust legislation for their profits.

But the case, even of the afflicted 50,000, is not so bad as it at first seems. Let us review their whole situation. Possessing 30 per cent. of all real-estate values, they enjoy an annual rent, from land and building, of close upon $700,000,000. Their income from tariff profits and the like has been put at $300,000,000. They would lose by the adoption of direct taxation only three per cent. of their rents; although they would lose, and ought to lose, the whole of the tribute which they levy upon their fellow citizens, by means of an abuse of the taxing power. The immense benefits which would be conferred upon the country, by the abolition of indirect taxation, would certainly increase rent by much more than three per cent.; and thus even this small class would lose nothing but the illegitimate profits, which they make by an abuse of the taxing powers of the national government.

Yet there must be some class which will lose absolutely by the concentration of taxes upon ground rents. There is. It is that small number of persons whose chief investment is in vacant land, and whose chief occupation is keeping land out of use.

§ 7. **The farmers.** In Great Britain and Ireland, no one who speaks of farmers thinks of men who *own* farms. And, indeed, the very word "farmer" signifies properly one who hires land from another. But, while we in the United States continued to use this English word, the totally different circumstances of our early history completely transformed its meaning. So vast a majority of those who tilled American farms owned their farms, in fee simple, that the name of farmer has, for long generations, necessarily implied the ownership of a farm. But little more than twenty years ago one of the best informed Americans, addressing an assembly of learned and distinguished Europeans, declared that the number of American farmers who did not own their farms was so small as to be entirely unworthy of consideration in the discussion of social or political questions.

This tradition still remains with us; and it is so ingrained in our ideas that in all discussions of public questions it is uniformly assumed, in good faith, that all American farmers are farm-owners. And no class appears to be more convinced of the truth of this assumption than farmers themselves. Indeed, so deeply rooted is this conviction in all their habits of thought, that, so far as can be judged from the public utterances of their especial representatives, American farmers are unanimously of opinion, not only that they all own their farms, but that they own substantially all the land in America, except a few thousand acres in a few large cities.

The inevitable consequence is that, in all discussions of taxation, the mass of American farmers take it for granted that every proposition to increase the share of taxation which falls upon the value of land is a proposition to increase their share of the public burdens; and up to this time all tillers of the soil have voted, with almost absolute unanimity, against every such proposal and in favor of every measure which even pretends to increase the burdens of taxation on buildings, improvements, and personal property.

The census of 1890 has struck a fatal blow to this illusion. It has demonstrated, as the figures now to be given will show, that more than one third of American farms are held by mere tenants (who are, almost always, tenants only from year to year), and that less than half of them are held by absolute owners, free of mortgage.

The official returns on this subject are as follows:

Ownership and Hiring of Farms.

Families owning, free............	2,255,789	
" " incumbered....	886,957	3,142,746
Families hiring.........................		1,624,433
Total......................		4,767,179
Families owning, free...........	2,255,789	
Families hiring or mortgaged.....	2,511,390	4,767,179

§ 8. **Farmers as a political factor.** In addition to the 1,600,000 landless farmers thus hiring farms, there must be taken into account fully 3,000,000 farm laborers, of voting age, who constitute part of the farming population, but who neither own nor hire farms. Thus the landless farm-voters number at least 4,600,000; while the land-owning farmers number only 3,100,000. Assuming that each of them is a voter, or the wife of a voter, the farm-owners constitute less than one fifth of the voting population.

The proportion of land values held by farmers shrinks when put to the test of statistics as much as does their numerical proportion. The same census returns the aggregate real value of farms at (in round numbers) $13,279,000,000, out of a total taxable real estate value of $46,000,000,000, including railroads, etc. As much more than one third of all farms are not owned by farmers, we must deduct at least one third from this farm value, in estimating the amount owned by farmers. This would leave them in possession of a value, in both land and its improvements, of about $8,800,000,000, or less than one fifth of the whole value of real estate, which closely corresponds with their proportion of the population.

The independent farmer, therefore, is a rapidly diminishing factor in American politics. He has had almost supreme power in his hands, in the past; and the result of his control of the government has been to put his class into a course of speedy extinction. Nevertheless, the interests of the farmers and farm-owners are entitled to full consideration; and they shall have it here. They, or those who assume to represent them, are the most clamorous opponents of intelligent and just taxation; and wherever they have control, they strenuously maintain a system of indiscriminate hodge-podge taxation, with its inevitable accompaniment of more perjury and more fraud to each cent collected than is attached to the collection of a dollar under even moderately scientific methods of taxation.

It has already been demonstrated, it is hoped, to the satisfaction of every intelligent reader, that the tax on personal property, to which the average farmer clings so tenaciously, only increases his share of taxes. But the effect of abolishing taxes upon buildings has been reserved, so far as the farmers' interest is concerned, for this place.

§ 9. **Do farm-owners gain by taxing improvements on land?** The farmer is apt to cry out against what he calls the injustice of exempting from all taxation the magnificent buildings sometimes erected in cities, forgetting that such buildings always stand upon the most expensive land, while his own farm house and barns stand upon land of utterly insignificant value. In adjusting taxation, *the only question of importance is as to the relative proportion which will be borne by different classes;* and it is of no importance whatever that any single piece of property should pay much or little, provided all other properties of the same kind pay in exact proportion with it. A farm house, costing $1,500 to build, will stand upon a piece of land which, including the surrounding garden, on an ample scale, would not be worth more than $15. But an average city house, costing $10,000 to build, will stand upon a lot worth at least $5,000; while a warehouse, costing $50,000 to build, will frequently stand upon a lot worth $50,000.

So far, therefore, as the mere value of land which is required for the purpose of supporting the house or building of any kind is concerned, the farmer would gain largely by concentrating taxes upon that and exempting all buildings.[1]

But he holds, in addition to the land upon which his house stands, a number of acres which he uses for farming purposes; and he assumes that these will be heavily taxed under a system of taxation upon land values alone, and that thus a larger proportion of the burden will be thrown upon him. This is an entire mistake. When buildings are exempt from taxation *all other improvements* on the land must also be exempted; and the result of this would be to assess improved farm lands at no higher

---

[1] Some readers may wish to see this statement proved in detail. Taking the illustrations from the text, and supposing a tax of $1165 to be laid upon the three pieces of property mentioned, the result, under the present system, would be as follows:

Farm house and land, $1515; city house and land, $15,000; warehouse and land, $100,000. Total, $116,515; tax rate, 1%. Tax on the farm house, $15.15, on the city house, $150, on the warehouse, $1000.

Under a system exempting all buildings and improvements, the assessment would be as follows:

Farm land, $15; city land, $5000; warehouse land, $50,000.

The gross tax remaining the same ($1165), it would be divided on a total assessment of only $55,015, requiring a tax rate of 2⅛%. The farm house owner would pay 32 cents; the city house owner, $106; the warehouse owner, $1059. *Reduction of farmer's tax,* 98 *per cent.*

value than perfectly wild, uncultivated land in the immediate vicinity. All fences, all growing crops, all improvements of every kind would be left out of account; and land would be assessed only at the value which it would bring if it had been just swept clean by a prairie fire. Very little consideration is required to enable any one to see that under such a rule of assessment the taxes levied upon farms would be much less, in proportion to those levied upon town lots, than they are to-day, and that such a change in the methods of assessment and taxation would result in lessening the burden of farmers and farm owners.

§ 10. **Proportion of improvements in farm values.** As, however, this point is most obstinately disputed, and statistics are constantly brought forward which upon their face indicate that improvements upon farms bear a much smaller proportion to land values than is the case in cities, the question needs further consideration. For, while we ought not to be affected by the mere fact that farmers constitute so large a portion of the voters in the United States as to give them a controlling influence in the decision of tax reforms, especially in view of their total failure in the past to exercise that power for their own good, we ought to give great weight to any evidence that an apparent reform would increase their burdens.

But the manifest tendency of wealth to concentrate in cities, the rapid rise in the value of city lands, and the stationary values of farm lands raise a strong presumption that land values bear a larger proportion to improvements in cities than in the country; and we may well distrust the correctness of any figures which indicate the contrary. Improvements, moreover, are merely items of personal property, which have been fastened to the land; and having seen that wealth in general flows into cities, we have good reason to doubt any statistics which seem to show that a disproportionate amount of one kind of personal property settles on farms. On the other hand, having seen that the taxation of movable chattels falls most heavily upon farmers, notwithstanding the universal expectation that it would not do so, we are prepared to find some similar miscalculation with respect to those immovable chattels which are called improvements upon land.

§ 11. **The true test.** Some assessments profess to separate the value of lands from the value of improvements. But it would seem, in all cases, that only *buildings* are reckoned as improvements; and it is certain that the value added to land, by drains, irrigation, and all the different forms of preparing land for cultivation, is never separately stated. It is true that much of this added value cannot now be distinguished, having been created so long ago that no estimate of it can fairly be made. But precisely the same thing is true of still more expensive improvements made in cities, paid for by local assessments in past years. Setting these aside, as balancing each other, farmers have a great advantage in certain universal tests, of easy and almost uniform application. Almost every farm has some land within its limits, or closely adjoining it, which is entirely unimproved, either never having been prepared for cultivation, or having lost all that had been done for that purpose. The value of this land will afford the proper measure for valuing the rest. The improved land should be estimated at no greater value than the unimproved. In the very few cases, in which every foot of ground in a farm is cultivated, the price which could be obtained for land taken out of an adjoining highway would afford as good a test. In the latter case due allowance would be made for the superior value attaching to such land, over the rest of the farm, by reason of its nearness to the road. The valuation would, in every case of farm assessments, be based on the market price of the land, as it would be if the soil had never been broken up or in any way prepared for use. The assessor would not inquire what was on the land fifty years before; but he would look at the surrounding land, under present conditions; and it would be his duty to reduce the valuation of land which had been broken up, plowed, fertilized, drained, cleared, and cultivated, to a level with other land, equally well or ill situated, for which nothing of the kind had been done.

At the present time, it is understood that Western wild land, which may be had for $5 an acre in its original state, sells for $15 when even fairly prepared for farming. A deduction of 66 per cent., therefore, would seem to be the lowest allowance required on this account. But this low rate is only applicable to land free from heavy stones, stumps of trees, and similar natural defects. The deduction to be made from the market value of lands which have been cleared from such defects, or which have been drained, irrigated or otherwise permanently improved, would be much greater. In Massachusetts cultivated farm land is worth, on an average, $55, while uncultivated but improvable land is worth only $15.[1]

As a matter of course, no assessment would be made upon the transient increase of value arising from fertilization, plowing, growing crops, fruit trees, or anything of that kind. To this extent the principle has been recognized in the new Constitution of California, which directs that cultivated and uncultivated land shall be assessed alike.

Upon the whole, it is safe to say that, under a system of valuation excluding all improvements, cultivated farms

[1] See Appendix to this chapter.

would be assessed at less than 40 per cent. of their whole value, improvements included.[1]

§ 12. **Comparison of farms with cities.** The case of cities stands in strong contrast. In no large city are buildings worth more than 50 per cent. of all real estate; while in Boston they are valued even by assessors at only 40 per cent. As under the present system vacant land is uniformly assessed much lower, in proportion to its market price, than is land covered by buildings, it is evident that the bare land of cities is worth much more than 60 per cent. of their real estate. From this value there can be no such deduction as is proper in the case of farms. Cultivation, crops, and fences add nothing to the market price of city lots. The cost of roads and other public improvements has not been deducted from the assessable value of farms; and therefore it must not be deducted from the value of city lots. If allowed in one instance, it must be allowed in the other; and in the end it would make little or no difference in the relative burden of taxation. It is better, therefore, to make no allowance for it in either case.

The result of a total exemption of improvements from taxation would thus appear to be a reduction of more than 50 per cent. in the taxable value of farms, and of less than 40 per cent. in the taxable value of cities. Of course, the reduction would be less in farms lying close to cities, and more in towns of small population, even though dignified with the titles of cities. Farms, when really held on speculation as town lots, are not entitled to rank with farms; and villages are not made cities, by labelling them as such.

Comparing *real* farms with *real* cities, the exemption of all personal property and improvements would reduce the taxation of farm owners in states having large towns by

[1] See Appendix to this chapter.

at least 30 per cent. For every $100 now paid by them they would then pay less than $70.[1]

Nor is this all which the farm owner would gain. Under the present system, an enormous amount of land value, in the form of railway, telegraph, telephone, gas-light and electric light franchises, goes untaxed. Most of this is found in cities and towns. All this would be taxed at its proper value, under the system which would immediately spring up if personal property and improvements were exempted; and the taxes thus collected would go in relief of farms. But this belongs to a later period of this discussion.

§ 13. **The farmers' loss and gain.** It having now been shown that taxes upon personal property and improvements of land bear more severely upon farmers than upon any other class of property owners in the United States, it only remains to give a summary statement of the general effect which the concentration of all taxes upon ground rents would have upon American farmers, taken as an entire class.

Using round numbers, it has been shown that the total ground rent of the United States for 1890 was $1,380,000,000; the whole amount of taxes to be provided for was $828,000,000; the local taxes on real estate were $354,000,000, and on personal property, $117,000,000; the national taxes, all indirect, were $358,000,000; while the burden of private profit or of waste, caused by the nature of indirect taxes, was about $700,000,000 in 1880, and could not well be less in 1890.

---

[1] This may be verified by comparing the assessments of Hamilton County (Cincinnati) and Medina County, Ohio (*Ante*, p. 90). It will be found that if these two counties were assessed on land values alone, estimating them at 60 per cent. of real estate in the city and 50 per cent. in the country, Medina's share would be fully 30 per cent. less than it is now.

It will not make much difference whether the farmers' share of land values in the United States is estimated at more or less than 30 per cent., since their proportion of local taxation will vary in proportion thereto. But according to the census of 1890 the value of farms was less than 30 per cent. of the value of all taxable real estate and land privileges.[1]

Farmers have never made any profit out of the higher prices caused by indirect taxation; and therefore they have paid their share of all profit so made, without receiving any part of it back.

Since American farms constituted, in 1890, 30 per cent. of all real estate, their owners must have paid at least 30 per cent. of the taxes on real estate. In fact they paid more; because land franchises did not pay their share. It has been demonstrated that they have always paid more than their proper share of taxes on personal property; and they have certainly paid at least one fourth of such taxes, taking the country at large.

Indirect taxes are of course paid, not in proportion to wealth or income, but according to consumption. If farmers live as well as other people, they pay such taxes in proportion to their numbers, not their property. It may be assumed that they are more frugal than most other land-owners. But farm *owners*, who form one fourth of all families, live in much better style than do the great mass of landless people. They therefore pay at least one-fourth of all indirect taxes. We thus reach the conclusions now stated.

American farm owners pay, under the present system of taxation:

---

[1] True value of all taxable real estate, over $46,000,000,000; of farms, $13,279,000,000.

30 % of taxes on real estate ($354,000,000)............... $106,200,000
25 % of taxes on personal property ($117,000,000)........... 29,250,000
25 % of indirect taxes and profits thereon ($1,050,000,000).... 262,500,000

$397,950,000

They would pay under the system here proposed:

30 per cent. of all necessary taxes, with no indirect burdens attached ($828,000,000)............................ $248,400,000

Reduction of Farmers' Taxes, through direct taxation........ $149,550,000

Thus the farmers would save much more than one third of their present tax burdens by the concentration of taxes on ground rents alone.

§ 14. **Relief of farmers, without injustice to others.** The question is naturally asked: "Since a certain sum must be raised, in any event, for the support of government, how can the burden of farmers as a class be lightened, without increasing to the same extent the burden of cities and towns?"

Of course, the proposal to collect taxes from only one source implies that the burden is to be increased upon the class which controls that source. But the proposal is that the whole burden shall be placed upon the *owners of ground rents*, including the franchises on land. Such owners form a very small minority of the residents of cities and towns; and therefore a vast majority of such residents would not suffer any increase of burdens, through any amount of relief which might be given to farmers. Town people will always pay most of the rent of every highly civilized country. They pay no less rent when the farmers are taxed heavily than they would pay if the farmers were not taxed at all. There is no conflict of interest between those who live in cities and those who live on farms. But there is a great conflict of interest between those who own city land and those who own the farms. Under a single tax upon ground rents, farm owners, as a class, would not pay nearly so large a share of taxes as they do now; because the value of their land is so much less than the value of city, town, and railway land. All that they would thus save would be cast upon the owners of city and town lots, or deducted from the excessive profits of monopolies. But the *tenants* of town property would gain fully as much as the *owners* of farms.

APPENDIX TO CHAPTER XII.

The census of Massachusetts for 1885 (the latest published) gives a full statement of the assessed value of farm property, distinguishing between improved land, unimproved land, unimprovable land, and buildings. The writer is not aware of the existence of any other statistics of this kind worthy of the least confidence. But these are evidently prepared honestly and intelligently, although large allowance must of course be made for errors.

This census showed the results of investigations into 45,010 separate farms or farm plots. On these " farms " (as it is most convenient to call them) there were 46,109 dwelling houses and 50,275 barns or other outbuildings. The average value of each farm was $2,459.47, of each house $1,009.76, and of each outbuilding $408.70.

The real estate of all farms was classified as follows:

Cultivated land....	939,260 acres....	$59,891,808	
Unimproved........	1,479,454 "	... 24,719,798	
Unimprovable.....	90,213 "	 809,892	
Woodland.........	1,389,502 "	 25,279,209	

Total land values....................... $110,700,707
Buildings............................... 74,418,218

Total value of land and buildings.......... $185,118,925

The average value per acre, for the entire State, of farm lands without buildings, was, for cultivated land, $63.76; for uncultivated, $16.26; for woodland, $18.17; for unimprovable, less than $9. But these values include land in cities, which of course was held for sale as town lots. Omitting land in cities, the average values were, for cultivated, $55.05; for uncultivated, $15.15; for woodland, $17.46.

Under the California rule, which would be followed under any system for the taxation of pure ground rents, the cultivated land would be assessed at no higher value than the other land. Assuming, however, that cultivated land is better situated than other land, and should therefore be valued about one third higher, say at $20 per acre, the total valuation of Massachusetts farm lands would have been, in 1885, about $69,594,100. This would have been the taxable value, instead of $185,118,925, which was the taxable value under the present system, so beloved by Massachusetts farmers.

The result of excepting all buildings and improvements from taxation would, therefore, be to reduce the assessment of farms 62 per cent. Or, to put it in the other way, farms would be assessed at only 38 per cent. of the present rate.

Now let us compare the reduction in the farm assessments which would be made under the tax on ground rents alone, with the reduction which would be made in city assessments as returned in 1890. The proportion has remained the same, substantially, for many years.

Boston and Brookline (which are territorially one) were assessed for $386,735,775 in land and $263,181,500 in buildings. There is no deduction to be made in cities on account of the non-cultivation of land. The pure land value of Boston was, therefore, 59½ per cent. of all its real estate; and the reduction in its assessment would be only 40½ per cent., as compared with 62 on the farms. The reduction to farms would thus be 50 per cent greater than the reduction in Boston. In Lowell, Springfield, and Worcester, which have within their limits a good deal of farm land,[1] the value of land and buildings are

---

[1] Farm land in Lowell, 3478 acres out of a total of 5989; in Springfield, 13,277 out of 16,807; in Worcester, 18,249 out of 20,835.

nearly equal. But even as against them, farms would have an advantage of 25 per cent. under the proposed system.

If all the taxes of Massachusetts were collected from real estate and divided between Boston and the farms, the farms would pay 45 per cent. *more*, under the present system of taxing both land and improvements, than they would pay under a tax upon the value of land alone.

No statement of the whole amount of personal property assessed upon Massachusetts farms alone is accessible. But by comparing three counties, Berkshire, Franklin, and Hampshire, in which the value of farms in 1885 constituted more than *half* the value of all real estate, with Suffolk County, in which farms constituted only the *one hundred and twentieth* part of real estate, we can reach a very fair conclusion as to the effect of the exemption of both personal property and improvements.

As we are compelled to compare the farm values of 1885 with the total assessments of 1890, there is no use in giving precise figures; and round numbers will therefore be used. The assessed value of all property in Suffolk County was $851,000,000. In the three farming counties it was $91,000,000. If personal property and buildings had been exempted, and land had been assessed at its unimproved value, the assessment of Suffolk would have been $377,000,000, and that of the three farming counties would have been less than $22,000,000. Thus the assessment of Suffolk County (which is only another name for Boston) would have been reduced 56 per cent.; but the assessment of the farming counties would have been reduced 76 per cent. Assuming the rate of taxation to be 1 per cent. on the present valuation, Boston would pay, under the present system, $8,510,000, and the farming counties, $910,000. Under the reformed system, Boston would pay $8,900,000, while the farming counties would pay only $520,000. The burden upon farms would be lightened by 43 per cent., and yet the burden of Boston would be increased by less than 5 per cent.; the State receiving precisely the same revenue, in any case. Or, to put it the other-way, Massachusetts farmers are paying 75 per cent. *more* of the State taxes, under the present system, than they would pay under a tax upon the unimproved value of land alone.

And still the Massachusetts farmers are clamorously demanding the perpetuation and extension of the very system which makes their burdens heavier, and would almost lose their senses if their taxes were reduced 40 per cent. by a rational system of taxation.

These statistics are taken from the Massachusetts " Census of agricultural products and property," for 1885, and the official " Aggregates of polls, property, and taxes," assessed in 1890. The census can be found in any good library. The other document can probably be obtained from the Secretary of State.

After the foregoing pages were in type, it was suggested by a critic, worthy of the highest respect, that these differences in value might be mainly the result of differences in site, nearness to markets, or inherent qualities of the land. But it will be found that this is not so. The Massachusetts census shows that about the same ratio of difference runs all through the State, in the towns nearest to markets as well as in those most distant, in the largest cities and in the smallest villages, on the hills and on the plains, where land is dear and where it is cheap. The allowance of twenty per cent. made above for the probable superiority of natural advantages possessed by cultivated land seems, upon close examination of the returns, to be ample.

Taking the three counties in Massachusetts where farms are of greatest importance compared with other investments, we find the average value per acre of all farm real estate, including buildings, of cultivated land, of pasture land capable of cultivation, and of all unimproved land, to run as follows :

Counties.	Real Estate.	Cultivated Land.	Pasture Land.	Unimproved Land.
Berkshire	$31 20	$38 87	$12 43	$11 19
Franklin	29 20	40 19	9 00	9 00
Hampshire	34 70	39 32	10 50	9 65

All land which is considered not worthy of improvement is excluded from pasture land. Yet it will be seen that, if improvements of all kinds were excluded from assessment, the real estate of farms in Berkshire County would be assessed at only 40 per cent., in Franklin County at only 33 per cent., and in Hampshire County at only 30 per cent. of the assessed value under the present system.

All these counties are within easy reach of good markets, but Franklin and Hampshire are especially so. Berkshire, on the other hand, has a much larger number of summer visitors, who are good customers for the season.

Selecting single towns, at the extremes of wealth, we find much the same results. In Berkshire County Stockbridge has the highest-priced land and Savoy the lowest-priced. In Stockbridge the average value of improved land is about $112 per acre, of unimproved land $49, and of land and buildings $118. In Savoy improved land is valued at about $7, land and buildings the same, and unimproved land at $2.87. Therefore, if assessments were made upon the value of unimproved land only, farms in wealthy Stockbridge would be assessed at 41 per cent. of their present rate, and in poor Savoy precisely the same.

The writer is well aware that statistics can be prepared from assessment rolls in other States showing apparently different results. He has carefully studied such returns from a dozen different States. If any of them had even pretended to give an extended statement of farm values, it should have been analyzed here. But not one of them does this; nor does one pretend to distinguish between buildings and other improvements. Almost without exception, they are admitted, by the officers issuing them, to be worthless. In Nebraska, the auditor states that the assessments are only about 5 per cent. of true values. In Illinois, they are about 12 to 15 per cent. If there were any uniformity in such undervaluations, the tables might still be useful; but there is none. These returns are simply monuments of the phenomenal incapacity or dishonesty of American assessors.

CHAPTER XIII.

Social Effects of Natural Taxation.

§ 1. **The effect in general.** The adoption of a natural, intelligent, and scientific system of taxation would bring about a just distribution of wealth, would give a perpetual stimulus to industry and production, would greatly increase wages, would increase the profits of capital, would give a security to property now unknown, would encourage manufactures, commerce, and agriculture, and would incidentally solve many social problems which under present conditions seem almost insoluble.

It is hoped that as each branch of the inquiry has been discussed, it has appeared that each step towards this great but simple reform has been attended with the solution of some difficult problem. But others have been reserved for this final review.

§ 2. **Stimulus to production.** It must surely be evident, without argument, that when all taxes are concentrated upon ground rents alone, and when every piece of land is estimated for assessment at the amount for which it could be rented for present use, the tax constantly increasing, in exact proportion to any increase in the rental value of the land, it would generally be impossible to hold any land out of use for the purpose of speculation. The only exception would be cases in which it was so clearly desirable that the land should be preserved for future use, that its possessor could better afford to pay the tax out of his capital than to allow the land to be put to any present use which would spoil it for a more desirable future use. The pressure put upon the land-owner to make immediate and beneficial use of the land would, in most cases, be irresistible. The result, in all but a few exceptional cases, would be that all land, which any one cared to claim as owner, would be put into immediate use for productive purposes; while a vast amount of land which is now held for pure speculation, would be abandoned to the use of any one who was willing to pay the annual tax.

Under such a system all land would be made useful, up to its full capacity. The possession of land would necessitate the constant employment of labor in its use and development; and all who were unable or unwilling to use land to the best advantage of the community would abandon it to those who were both able and willing.

But this is only one of the many stimulants to production which are involved in reformed taxation. Think of the many other encouragements which industry would receive. Money and credit, free from all taxes, would crowd into the industrial field. Factories, mills, furnaces, foundries, workshops, stores, offices, machinery, tools, instruments of production in every conceivable form, would all be free from taxes. The farmers' barns, crops, plows, tools and implements, his horses, cattle, sheep, materials and products of every kind, would be free of tax. His land could be drained, stubbed, subsoiled and improved to the highest point, without adding a dollar to his taxes. Commerce would be free as air. The farmer would buy in the cheapest market, and sell in the dearest. Monopoly could no longer hinder production. The only limit of production would be the limit of demand.

§ 3. **Effect on wages.** Using the term "wages" as including all forms of compensation for personal labor, it should seem clear that the great increase in production which would thus be brought about must greatly increase the demand for labor, and would therefore produce a general and permanent advance in wages.

Nominal wages, expressed in terms of money, must advance, because there would be an anxious demand for labor on the part of all land-owners. For without a constant supply of efficient labor, the annual tax could not be paid; and then the land would fall into the hands of those who would extract from the land, either by their own labor or by the labor of others, a revenue sufficient to pay the tax, with a profit. The increased demand for labor thus arising would, in any country large enough to make a rate of its own, largely increase the general rate of wages. That this is the invariable result, in all similar cases, has been abundantly proved by past experience. The opening of new land to labor has always tended to increase wages; and under the proposed system of taxation there would be an enormous increase in the new land thus opened to labor, and therefore a corresponding increase in the reward of labor. The effect upon wages would be precisely that which would be produced by the discovery of a new continent of fertile and healthy land.

Real wages (in other words, the real reward of labor) would be increased to a much greater extent than *nominal* wages. For while wages, expressed in forms of money, must rise, as already shown, prices of the good things which wages buy would fall, on account of the much greater production of such things, which would result from the immensely greater application of labor and capital to land. More than this, it having been already shown that the bulk of taxation is now borne by the wage-earners, and that the whole of this taxation would be taken off their shoulders by the new system, their *real* income would be practically increased by the full amount of this reduction of taxation ; the effect of which they would feel in a general reduction of the cost of living.

§ 4. **Effect on money wages.** The advance in money wages must, of necessity, be rather vaguely estimated. But long experience has furnished abundant means for trustworthy calculations. It is not at all necessary that there should be a demand for double the number of laborers, to double the rate of wages. A much smaller increase in the demand will suffice, so long as the supply of labor does not meet the demand.

It having been shown that the taxation of ground rents would compel their owners to employ labor in producing something, out of which taxes could be paid, while the release of the great purchasing class from heavy taxation would enlarge their purchasing power, it follows that an immediate demand for labor would arise, in excess of the local supply. The degree to which wages would rise, in consequence of this demand, would largely depend upon the extent of the field over which the new system of taxation was in force. The adoption of just taxation in a single county, or even in an entire State, would cause a great increase of production there; but wages would be kept down, to a considerable degree, by the incoming of laborers from outside.

§ 5. **Immigration and wages.** But the adoption of just taxation, throughout the United States, would cause a rise in wages far too great to be repressed by foreign immigration. Laborers of all kinds have never yet come to America, in any one year, to the extent of even one twentieth part of the home supply. As the new arrivals furnish a market for nearly all that they earn, they do not, at the utmost, furnish an element of competition with native laborers in excess of one half of their earnings.[1] If, therefore, the average rate of American wages could be doubled, by causes having a permanent operation, immigration might continue at full tide, for many years, before it could seriously affect wages. The truth of this theory may be illustrated by the case of domestic servants. From various causes their average wages in the United States have much more than doubled since 1860. Those who then received $6 a month could now readily earn $14, while living in much greater comfort and having much easier work. The immigration of women of this class has been enormous; but it has never reduced wages. It may well be doubted whether it has even had any material influence in preventing a further advance. All the great advance in the wages of domestic servants has occurred since they began to arrive in great numbers.

We may safely assume that any rise in wages which would result from a reform in taxation, extending over the whole or the larger portion of the United States, would be permanent, notwithstanding any probable amount of immigration.

§ 6. **Amount of rise in wages.** As the purchasing power of laborers would be increased at least 15 per cent. from the instant at which taxes were taken off their purchases, an increase of demand to that extent may be assumed as certain, subject to such reduction of demand as might be caused by the reduced profits of the not more than 50,000 families, who would suffer any loss of in-

[1] Thus, suppose 800,000 immigrants to arrive in one year, less than half of them would be competitors for wages. Suppose the 400,000 competing laborers to earn $400 each. They would spend $350 of this. Half of this would be paid in wages to other laborers, producing what the new-comers wanted. Even if the other half injuriously affected resident laborers, it would amount to less than one cent in each dollar of their annual wages.

come through the new taxation. As their losses would not trench upon their usual fund for expenditure, their purchases would fall off only to a very moderate degree. An allowance of $3000 for each of these families would be ample. This would amount in all to $150,000,000, or not more than one tenth of the increase in the purchasing power of the other classes. After making large allowance for a saving disposition among the poorer classes, under their new prosperity, it is impossible to estimate the increase in purchases at less than ten per cent., or 1,000,000,000 per annum. It would probably be much more.

On the other hand, the anxiety of land-owners to put their land to profitable use, the absolute release of all productive industry from burdens, shackles, and restrictions, the untaxed money, untaxed manufactures, untaxed commerce, untaxed agriculture and untaxed credit would all combine to give a sudden and tremendous stimulus to industry. Production, for these reasons alone, could not fail to increase immensely. Adding this consideration to the other, the effective demand for labor could not fail to increase by more than one third; and this would cause a rise in wages of fully 100 per cent.

§ 7. **Effect on capital.** The owners of capital will naturally desire to know how their interests will be affected. Will not the doubling of wages diminish the profit of capital? No. On the contrary it will greatly increase that profit.

In the first place, it must be remembered that ground rents are *not* capital. Correctly speaking, they are not even true wealth. They are mere taxes upon wealth—instruments by which tribute can be exacted from wealth. We are now considering only genuine capital—true wealth, employed in the reproduction of wealth.

In the next place, capital necessarily depends for its

profit upon a large demand for its productions. Modern capitalists are fully aware that great gains can never come from small transactions, no matter how large the profit on each transaction may be. Sales of $1,000,000 at a profit of 50 per cent. are of small account, compared with sales of $100,000,000 at a profit of 5 per cent. The number of those who live without their own labor is and must be always and everywhere so small, compared with the vast mass of mankind, as to afford an insignificant market for the enormous production of modern industry. The vast majority, who labor with their own hands, furnish the only market worthy of consideration for modern capital.

This great majority always spend the larger part of their earnings ; and they would continue to do so, even if their earnings were doubled or trebled. The doubling of their wages means, therefore, the doubling of the market for the joint production of labor and capital. It means the doubling of the gross profit of capital. This would not be true of a similar increase of income to any other class. The owners of rent would not double their purchases, if rent were doubled. They would put much of their surplus into capital, competing with capital already invested. This might be good for others than capitalists. Yet, unless it brought about an increase of wages, it would not increase the demand for goods ; and so it would not increase the profit of capital. An increase of wealth, in the hands of the few, leads to increased wastefulness in the nature of their expenditures. Their outlay does not reproduce capital. The outlay of the working classes does. Not only does their food renew their vigor, but even their amusements, when intelligently directed, greatly increase their productive power and energy. High wages lead not only to cheap production, but also to a vast increase of production. They also lead immediately to a corresponding increase of the market for such productions.

There is no conflict of interest between labor and capital; although there are many conflicts of interest between individual laborers and individual capitalists. The lifting of all taxation from labor and capital will benefit both.

§ 8. **Absolute security of property.** When taxation is levied exclusively upon ground rent every man will have, for the first time in human history, an absolute and indefeasible title to all of his property which is the production of human skill and industry, subject only to the right of the state to take it, upon making full compensation for its value. Such compensation would enable the owner to replace the property thus taken with other property of the same description and value. This general right of the state is practically no limitation upon the absolute right to individual property.

It is perfectly plain that no one has any such right at present, and that no one can have it, under any existing system of taxation. For, so long as the state assumes the right to tax any thing besides rent, it is impossible for any man to retain the entire fruits of his own industry. Every year the state will deduct something from those fruits, under the name of taxation; and no one can ever foresee precisely how much will be taken in this manner. The fluctuations, both in the amounts and methods of such taxes, are so great and incalculable, that no one can have any reasonable certainty as to the extent to which his earnings will be secure against the demands of the state.

But if taxes were once confined strictly to ground rent, all this would be changed. Chattels of every description would of course be absolutely secure; since the only remedy which would be allowed to the state for the collection of taxes would be a sale of some exclusive privilege on land. But buildings and all other improvements on land would be equally secure against all taking *without compensation*. This is not at first sight so clear; and it needs, therefore, fuller explanation.

§ 9. **Improvements paid for our tax sales.** The exclusive tax upon ground rent would lose its entire character if the state were allowed, under any pretence, to collect it from personal property or improvements. It is a fundamental condition of such a tax that it be collected *only out of rent*. It must, therefore, when payment is refused, be collected only by selling the control of the taxed land to some person, who will not only pay the tax, but will also pay to the landholder, thus sold out, the full value of all his improvements. If no one will pay the tax, subject to those conditions, that is conclusive proof that the tax is too high, and that it is in reality based upon an assessment including other values than the mere value of the land. The purchaser in such case would, of course, take the land, subject to the annual liability for taxes; but he would also acquire the same absolute title to improvements which the previous possessor had; so that he, in turn, could not be sold out for taxes without full compensation for improvements. Thus no one would ever pay taxes upon the value of any other property than the bare land.

Universal experience has demonstrated that there would not be the slightest difficulty in carrying such a system into practical operation. This system has long been in operation, upon a great scale, both in public and private affairs. Wherever ferry franchises belong to a municipality, as in the city of New York, such franchises are sold at auction, at intervals of five or ten years, always subject to two conditions: first, the payment of rent to the municipality; and second, the payment of full compensation to the former holder of the franchises, for boats, piers, houses, and all other structures and materials used in operating the ferry. Street railroad franchises are sold in the same manner, for terms of years, by every *honest* municipal body having control of the subject.[1] So landlords constantly lease their land for terms of years, to men who erect expensive buildings thereon; the landlords covenanting to pay the value of such improvements upon the expiration of the lease. There is no more difficulty in providing for an annual sale of land, if necessary, subject to these conditions, than there is in providing for a sale in every five, ten, or twenty years. A ferry franchise is just as much a title to " land," within the meaning of law, science and common sense, as is any other land title whatever.[2]

Of course the valuation of improvements would be made upon a common-sense basis. The land-owner, upon making default in taxes, would be entitled to just as much compensation for his buildings as those buildings really added to the market value of the land on which they were built, but no more. If, as often happens, an expensive building had been put up in a district where it could never be of any use, nothing should be allowed for it beyond the value of its materials, after it had been pulled down. But for any really useful building, compensation would be allowed, sufficient to enable the owner to put up a similar building, in similar condition, upon an adjoining tract of land. In short, whatever loss the owner of the

[1] The conception of a really incorruptible city council will seem, to most American readers, too wildly improbable for the basis of even a theory. But effete Europe is so far behind us, in the grand march of civilization, that such Utopian bodies are quite common there.; and the method of the text is common also.

[2] Benson *v.* New York, 10 Barbour, 223. 233.

building incurred, by reason of his own mistakes or extravagance, he would be left to bear; but whatever value belonged to the building, exclusive of the land underneath it, he would invariably be allowed to retain.

§ 10. **The railway problem.** This is no place for even a full statement of the great railway problem, with its almost endless branches. Much less will an attempt be here made to give it a complete solution. All that will be attempted is to suggest the close connection between this complicated problem and the simple one of taxation.

It is by no means so clear as it seems to those who suffer from them, that high railway rates are actually unjust. That which *is* unjust in such cases is generally the fact that the large profits made upon such transactions are in the nature of rent, and equitably belong to the whole community. All attempts to correct this apparent injustice have thus far failed; and it may be worthy of inquiry whether this failure is not caused by some unrecognized justice in the system complained of. May it not be, that the wrong consists, not in the differential rates, but in the failure of the government to collect any part of these differences for public use?

Are not many of the evils complained of due to inflated nominal values and fictitious securities? That such is the general opinion, is strongly indicated by the stringent prohibition of fictitious stocks and bonds, in the new constitutions of Illinois, Pennsylvania, and other States, as well as in the statutes of still more. But if this opinion is well founded, the concentration of taxes upon land privileges, including railway franchises, will practically settle that question, by taking a very large part of such inflated values for public use.

The complete separation between the ownership of the road and the ownership of moving stock, proposed by

Mr. Hudson,[1] would seem to cover all the remaining ground. Under the one natural tax, the owners of the road would be taxed in proportion to the value of its franchise; but the owners of rolling stock would not be taxed at all. All persons and corporations could operate trains upon the road, subject to general rules. If the people of any place were charged too much for the carriage of their persons or property, they could put their own trains upon the road, on equal terms with all others. This was the original railway idea; and it has been abandoned, not because it is really impracticable, as railway managers pretend, but because it is less profitable to railway companies than the monopoly which is created by the present system.

§ 11. **Just taxation the remedy for unjust appropriation.** The proposal of a method of just scientific, and natural taxation is so simple and unpretending, that eager social reformers cannot believe it possible that it can carry with it any cure for the evils of our time. They point to the unequal distribution of wealth, the growth and powers of monopolies, the watered stocks and bonds, the bribe-bought franchises, the usurped privileges, the stolen lands, the wholesale appropriation of public property to private use; and they ask how it can be possible that "a mere fiscal reform" can bring relief from any of these evils. Yet it can. No great upheaval of society is needed. No social re-organization is required. No general state assumption of the machinery of production is either necessary or desirable.

It is continually but erroneously denied that the enormous fortunes of the present day are due to land monopoly or to methods of taxation. Fortunes of considerable

---

[1] *The Railways and the Republic.*

extent are gained by skill and genius; and there is no good reason why such fortunes should not be encouraged. Bessemer, Edison, Bell and other inventors have deserved wealth; and the capitalists, who made their inventions possible and forced them upon public attention, deserve it too. But all the unwieldy fortunes, and all which have had an undesirable origin, owe their existence to some form of monopoly, which could not have existed under the natural system of taxation.

The enormous wealth of British dukes and of our own —or lately our own—Astors, is of course due entirely to the comparative exemption of ground rents from taxation. But all the excess of wealth gained by railway kings, above a liberal compensation for shrewdness, sagacity, and foresight, is due to precisely the same cause. It has been shown that the chief value of railways consists in exclusive and peculiar privileges upon land; and the greatest part of this value arises from its comparative exemption from taxation.

The great monopolies, which have grown with such startling rapidity, into such overshadowing power, owe all their wealth and power to their manipulation of railways and of duties on imports. Under natural taxation there would be no import duties to manipulate; and railways could not afford to be manipulated.

§ 12. "**Watered stocks.**" Let us pass to the consideration of the inflated stocks and bonds, which are made the excuse for extortion. What can taxation do with them? The answer is so plain that one wonders at the question. Even without the adoption of the full reform here proposed, the change of a few lines in the tax laws would put a speedy end to these abuses. If all corporate securities were made subject to the general tax rate, at their full nominal value, the "water" would be let out of them within three months. "Yet show I unto you a more excellent way."

Stock inflation does not really enable railways to charge high rates. The Erie line cannot charge more on through traffic than the Central. And, upon the whole, those who use railways do not pay more than the service is worth. The real evil is that a very great part of the value of such service consists in the use of the land over which the railway runs, that this portion belongs to the public, and that hardly any of it is taken, as it ought to be, for public use. The proper remedy is not to give service to those who use the railways, for less than it is worth, but to use the same share of the value of railway land for public purposes, as in the case of other lands. When this is done, the entire people will receive through relief from other taxation their share of the value which they have given to the railways. And, at the same time, it will become impossible for railway companies to maintain inflated stocks and bonds; because to do so would be to invite greater taxation than they could bear.

§ 13. **Corrupt grants.** So as to bribe-bought franchises. It would be quite unnecessary to *rescind* them. It would only be necessary to *tax* them on the basis of their true value, which is pure ground rent. Thus American street railroads, which generally owe their franchises to the grossest corruption, and which charge fares of five or ten cents for a service which costs less than half that sum, need not be interfered with. Under a proper system of taxation, it would make little difference whether the fares were reduced or not. If the fares were reduced to three cents, ground rents would be increased, and the city would derive greater revenue from its taxes on those rents. If the fares remain unchanged, the value of the railroad franchise would be so much greater, and the tax upon that would be greater in proportion. It would make little difference, even to those who travelled in the cars. If the fares were reduced, the travellers would have to pay more rent for their homes. Thus they would contribute as much to the public funds in one way as in the other.

At first sight it would seem that the redress thus obtained would be very inadequate. But it would not. Of course, no past wrong can be entirely obliterated. No scheme of social reform seriously proposes to secure compensation for all the past. The world does not contain wealth enough to pay damages for all past injuries. But the taxation of all franchises, on the basis of their present fair market value, with the concentration of all taxes upon ground rents, of which these are a part, would take for the public benefit all that the public could have secured, under the most honest and impartial sale of such franchises. It will also tax those corporations which obtained their grants for nothing, just so much more than it will tax those which paid a fair price.

§ 14. **Taxation the best remedy for past corruption.** For these franchises could not, upon the average, have been originally sold for more than they would now pay under such taxation. If they had been sold at auction, for a sum in cash, free of taxation, they would never have brought a sum which, however well invested, would produce an income equal to the average annual tax. If new franchises should be sold, free of taxation, to the highest bidder for an annual payment, that payment, in the long run, would rarely, if ever, equal the taxes which would be paid under this system. Therefore it would be better, in the long run, to give these franchises to the corporations which will give the best security for the best and cheapest public service, than to sell them to the highest bidder, either for a single or an annual payment. Indeed, to sell them for a single present payment is obviously a bad method. It confines competition to a very few men of great wealth, depriving the municipality of the better service, which less wealthy but more energetic men would probably render; it cripples the operation of the franchise by impairing the capital of the managers; and it pours into the public treasury a large sum, which cannot be well invested, and which is an almost irresistible temptation to extravagance and waste.

And those corporations which have obtained valuable franchises for nothing, except bribes, will necessarily be taxed more heavily than those which are already subject to an annual payment. Thus the Broadway Railroad, in New York city, is subject to an annual payment of $40,000. The real annual value of its franchise (obtained by paying aldermen $20,000 each) is so much more than $400,000, that this figure may be taken, as an extremely moderate one. Assuming that to be correct, the taxable value of this franchise would be reduced to $360,000, by this liability to an annual payment. If another charter, equally valuable, should be granted in a parallel street, for nothing, its taxable value would be the full $400,000. Supposing half of such values to be taken by taxation, half the amount gained by bribery would be recovered. Under the present system, every conceivable method for recovering the loss sustained by the community through such schemes of corruption has been tried, without the slightest success. Even if the adoption of just taxation should only recover half of a just compensation for the franchises corruptly given away, that is a thousand times more than has ever yet been recovered, and ten times more than ever can be recovered in any other way.

§ 15. **Usurped lands.** Take the case of usurped or stolen lands. In Great Britain, the lords of the manor, having had control of Parliament for centuries, have stolen vast quantities of land from the people, under the forms of law. In the United States, vast tracts of land have been taken up, under forged grants or under perjured testimony. Spanish grants are a by-word; and the homestead law has been perverted into the most successful scheme for buying government land at a fourth of its value, which could have been devised. It ought to be entitled: "An Act to prohibit the purchase of land by honest men, and to encourage monopoly and perjury." Railroad lands, to the amount of hundreds of millions of acres, have been obtained for nothing, except a few beggarly bribes to Congressmen and State legislators, amounting in all to less than a ten thousandth part of the market value. What then? Shall we sue in the courts for relief? None could be had, without laying down rules of law, which would be ruinous to innocent purchasers, all over the land. Shall we pass confiscatory laws? The Constitution forbids; and if it did not, our own consciences would revolt at the idea. There is no possible relief in that direction.

Great Britain has no written constitution; and her Parliament has unlimited power. Shall Parliament direct the confiscation of the old common lands? Shall it undertake to reclaim literal possession of "the land for the people"? Let us not waste time in discussing the question on moral grounds. Rightly or wrongly, the moral sense of the people would revolt at such a proposition. And if it did not, yet the immense complications involved in awarding compensation for improvements would break down the whole project. It is not worth while to inquire into the abstract morality of an utterly impracticable scheme,

But, in Great Britain and America alike, the adoption of a just, natural, and uniform method of taxation would give an immediate remedy. Without confiscation, without violence, without any social upheaval, it would take for public use about half of the revenue thus misappropriated, which is no more than ought to be taken, in any case; while it is far more than can ever be obtained in any other way.

"The best remedy for injustice is simple justice."

§ 16. **Reform in government.** By this time, it is hoped, the attentive reader will have begun to see that the adoption of natural taxation leads, by an easy course, to reform in all methods of government and the abolition of corruption in public office, by removing most inducements to corruption. It would nearly extirpate the bribery of legislatures and councils, by leaving nothing for any one to gain by offering bribes. Not absolutely, of course. It cannot be too often repeated, that nothing in this world is or ever will be perfect. But this reform in taxation would remove most of the present inducements to bribery, falsehood and fraud in public affairs.

§ 17. **Abolition of fraud and bribery in tax matters.** The most prolific sources of these evils are directly connected with bad methods of taxation. Every change in laws imposing taxes upon commodities, either by a tariff or by excises, affects so many private interests that all parties agree in charging wholesale bribery and corruption upon each other, and none seriously claim to be innocent. This branch of the subject has already been sufficiently treated. The innumerable frauds and perjuries which arise out of the taxation of personal property have also been referred to. All these abominations would disappear, with the acceptance of natural taxation. Nobody would be required to make any return of his wealth;

and no attention would be paid to it, if he made any.
There would be but one thing to be taxed ; and its value
would be ascertained by independent investigation. Valuations of land might be compared with the rents actually
paid; but those rents would be learned by inquiry among
tenants, not among landlords. Large land-owners might
attempt to bribe assessors, as they do now. But the
value of land is so easily determined, that other landowners could be provided with an ample remedy, in an
application to the courts to make assessments just and
uniform.

§ 18. **Special local assessments dispensed with.**
The complex system of special assessments for local
improvements, which is indispensable under all existing
methods of taxation, with its allowance for "betterments," to use a current English term, would become
unnecessary. All improvements could be made at the
common expense; because whatever improvement might
thus be made in the value of adjoining property would
all be an increase in the value of the mere land ; and this
addition would lead at once to a permanent increase in
the tax upon that land, to a proportionate amount. Such
assessments have always been a fertile source of injustice,
inequality, and fraud. They are, inevitably, largely based
upon guesswork ; whereas the subsequent taxation would
be measured by actual, known values.

§ 19. **Bribery made unprofitable.** The most appalling
developments of crime in American government, however, have taken place with regard to the grants of special
privileges on land, especially to railway, gas, electric light,
and similar companies. The notorious robbery of the
United States by the Union Pacific and Central Pacific
companies, to an amount exceeding $100,000,000, is only
one of many instances, although the most prominent one.

The repeated purchase of the Broadway Railroad franchise from corrupt aldermen and legislators, repeatedly set aside by the courts, has attracted more attention than hundreds of similar crimes. But every street railroad franchise in New York has certainly been procured in precisely the same way; and probably every such railroad in the country, the franchise of which was worth anything, was chartered upon similar terms. Gas companies, electric light companies and steam heating companies, all pay heavy bribes for permission to lay their pipes or wires in city streets.

The taxation of all these franchises, at their full value, on the same basis with other privileges over land, would make it impossible to obtain them for nothing. No bargains with aldermen could relieve them from paying handsomely for their annual value. There would no longer be an eager crowd of bribe-offerers; and therefore the crowd of bribe-takers would cease to buy their way into municipal government. The bribes offered to aldermen would be too small to repay the aldermen's bribes to their electors. Such franchises would be generally given to those who would accept them on terms most favorable to the public, with respect to low charges, good accommodation, and faithful service. No money would be paid, either to the municipality or to the aldermen; for taxes would have to be paid; and they would automatically increase, as the value of the franchises increased.

§ 20. **The tenement house problem.** The rapid increase of low-class tenement houses in large American cities, especially in New York, has excited the just anxiety and alarm of our most thoughtful citizens. Many plans of restriction and regulation are urged. They all aim at results which are eminently desirable. But they all involve large expenses, which must be finally borne, under our present methods of taxation, by the very tenants whose extreme and degrading poverty is the very cause of the difficulty. It is perfectly true that such houses do not afford sufficient space and air to sustain health. It is often true that they do not furnish accommodations necessary to maintain decency; although much has been done of late years to improve them and to keep them under careful inspection. But every good thing is costly; and who is to pay the cost? If the landlord is forced by law to provide better accommodations, he must charge more rent for the house; and it has been already shown that he can, in the long run, compel the payment of such additional rent; because, if he could not, no more tenement houses would be built until tenants were able and willing to pay a fair rate of interest upon all the cost of building such houses, including all compulsory improvements.

Or suppose that the cost of such improvements is paid by the government. The expense would be paid out of taxes. Who would pay the taxes? A full share would fall upon these very houses; and, as the cost of such improvements when made by the city would be far greater than it would be if they were made by the landlord, the probability is that the tax upon the class of houses thus State-repaired would be nearly as great as the cost of private repair would be. Be it more or less, this tax must be finally paid by the tenants. And in this event, a large share of the tax would fall upon other buildings, occupied by a class but little less poor than the occupants of tenement houses; and thus they would be dragged down into actual poverty.

The next result would be that the tenement dwellers would be so impoverished by the increase of their rents, as to deprive them of some portion of the food or clothing, which they had with difficulty managed to provide under the original rent. All of them would suffer inconvenience; most of them would suffer actual privation; their earning power would be reduced; and many of them would be driven out altogether, by the bidding of other tenants, who had previously occupied houses or parts of houses of a slightly higher grade, which they had been compelled to give up by the pressure of taxation, or which, while they were much better than the tenements had been before tenements were reformed, were no better than the reformed and improved tenements.

Any compulsory improvements of this kind must inevitably make the lot of the lower class—the "residuum," as it is called—harder than ever.

As usual, it will be said that "this is all theory." Unfortunately it is a theory which was never much thought of, until practical experience called attention to it. The dwellings of the poor have been torn down and rebuilt with improvements, upon a large scale, in Paris, London, Berlin and other cities, and always with precisely these results. Those who occupied the old, condemned buildings did not return to the new ones. They simply could not afford it. Their places were taken by others, who had always occupied rather better homes, and who were driven by increased taxation to descend a step in the social scale, finding in the new dwellings, homes not quite equal to their old abodes, but much better and more expensive than the buildings which had been destroyed as unhabitable. The "residuum" were driven into more degraded conditions than those under which they previously lived.

§ 21. **Its solution.** Must we then abandon all hope of improvement in the homes of the poor? Not at all. While insisting upon renovations and necessary improvements, *let us remove all taxes from houses.* This will make houses more abundant; this will make house rents cheaper; this will enable house owners to furnish necessary improvements, without increasing rents or losing interest on their investments.

Let us work out an illustration. Twenty thousand dollars is a reasonable estimate for the price of many tenement houses in New York; half for the house and half for the land. Houses being usually assessed for 70 per cent. of their full value, the house, as distinguished from the land, would be assessed at $7000, and taxed, at present rates, $133. If this tax were taken off, representing, as it does, a capital of about $2600, the owner could afford to spend $2000 on improvements without raising the rent, and yet make a profit. Competition with other house owners would eventually compel him either to spend about as much or else to reduce his charge for the house by more than $100 a year. Legislation might hasten his action or require him to make the improvements, instead of lowering his rent. In either case the tenants' condition would be greatly improved.

Without deciding that no other reform is necessary or desirable, it is at least demonstrated by long and wide experience that no permanent and complete reform of the tenement house is possible, without first abolishing all taxes on buildings.

§ 22. **Summary of conclusions.** The adoption of natural taxation would obviously relieve the great mass of the people from all taxes and tax-burdens whatever, except rent ; which they now pay, in addition to taxes.

It would put an end to that artificial concentration of wealth in the hands of a few, which is now making such rapid progress.

While leaving natural inequalities in human skill, intelligence, industry, and productive power to produce their natural effects, in moderate inequalities of wealth, it would gradually remove those unnatural and monstrous inequalities which now exist, with no benefit to any one and with vast injury to society as a whole.

It would put a premium upon improvement and industry, by relieving them from double taxation; while it would lay such burdens upon mere "dogs in the manger," as would drive them into productive industry.

It would secure to the owner of every product of human industry and skill an absolute and indefeasible title to such property; so that it could not be taken from him, even for taxes, without full compensation for its market value; a title, therefore, far superior to any which can now be held by any human being.

It would increase the demand for human labor in the production of good things for human use, to the utmost possible limit; thus causing a general rise in wages of at least 50 per cent. and more probably 100 per cent.

It would relieve wages from all present forms of taxation; thus increasing the net income of laborers, at once and forever, by at least 15 per cent. more. Whether "times" were good or bad, wages high or low, the net income of every laborer would always be *at least* 15 per cent. higher than it could possibly be under the present system, at similar periods.

It would encourage capital to free investment, by relieving it from all fear of punishment for enterprise, under the name of taxation.

It would solve the American currency problem, by opening banks of deposit in every nook and corner, free of taxation; thus giving to every farmer precisely the same facilities for exchange as are enjoyed by the wealthiest merchant or manufacturer, and making a large supply of either coin or notes superfluous.

It would largely reduce the share of taxes paid by farmers, because their share of ground rent is smaller than is that of other land owners ; while it would not increase the present burdens upon residents of towns and cities, since they would pay nothing but rent ; and that they pay now, in addition to taxes.

It would remove all shackles from commerce, trade, manufactures, agriculture, and industry of every kind, giving them a stimulus such as they have never known.

It would throw open to all men some land, upon which they could make a living, without requiring them to invest any capital in its purchase, and at no greater rent than they could reasonably afford to pay.

It would, therefore, enormously increase the production and wealth of the nation, while securing a fair, though not literally equal, distribution of that wealth.

It would reform government, by lifting the masses out of the degrading conditions which make them an easy prey to corrupt influences, by removing all temptation to fraud in matters of taxation, and by destroying the chief inducements to the corruption of legislatures and councils.

It would not at once make men moral, industrious, or intelligent; it would not give to any man a dollar which he did not earn for himself; it would not open any "royal roads" to wealth ; for " royal " ways are ways of idleness.

But it would open fair and equal opportunities to men of equal capacity and industry; and it would remove nearly all artificial hindrances to the success of the honest, intelligent, and industrious.

INDEX.

Ad valorem taxes, 22
Andrews, George H., 75
Argyll, Duke of, 129
Assessment, of personal property, how made, 63–69
  of merchandise, 64, 65–68
  of furniture, 64, 65
  by donkey race, 69
  methods in Rhode Island and Rome, 69
  of buildings and improvements, 110–114
  of ground rent, 121
  of unimproved value of farm lands, 122
  judicial correction of, 123
  correction of, by sales, 123, 124
  of franchises, 125–128
    now omitted, 154, 155
  for local improvements, 217
Astor family, 166, 211
Astor, Mrs. W. W., commended, 20
Atkinson, Edward, 137, 139, 152, 154
  on Boston rents, 137, 152, 154
Automatic taxation, 115

Bad taxation, effects of, 3, 4
  what is, 4, 5
  causes currency trouble, 60–62
Bank deposits, not money, 57
  mere credits, 57

Banks, taxation of, 60–62
    a success, 60
    a disaster, 60
    cause of currency troubles, 60–62
  scarce in Southwest, 61
  abundant in Scotland and Canada, 62
Boston, personal property tax in, 81–83
  ground rent in, 137, 138, 152–157
  taxes in, 138, 152, 153, 156
Bribery. See *Corruption*
Brooklyn, income tax in, 31
  taxes on houses in, 111
Buildings, taxes on, 106–114. See *Improvements*
Burden of taxation, under present system, 24–27
    private profits, 24–27
    amount of, 27
    where it falls, 35
  on personal property, 63–69, 75, 78, 84–87, 88–105
    of farmers, 63–65, 84–100. See *Farmers*
    of merchants, 64–68. See *Merchants*
    of women and children, 101–105. See *Women*
  on buildings and improvements, 113, 114
  of farmers, 185–198
  under natural system, 174–198
    amount of, 174
    on landless, 177
    on land-owners, 177–182
    on vacant lands, 182
    on farmers, 182–194. See *Farmers*
  See *Incidence of taxation*

California, taxation in, 76–81
  no butter, wool, or honey in, 77
  money leaving, 77, 79
  assessments in, 79, 80, 122
  merchandise, bonds, and credits in, 80

California, failure of personal property tax in, 76-78
   original government and taxation in, 167
Capital, effect of natural taxation on, 204-206
Chattels, what are? 50
   visible, taxation of, 62-69
      farmers hold most, 63-65
      assessment of, 64-69
Chicago, unequal assessments in, 113
Class legislation, 169
Collection of taxes, methods iniquitous, 18-22
   use of spies in, 19, 22
   enormous penalties in, 19, 22
Compensation, for taxation, 170
   for vested rights, 171-173
Concentration of wealth, how progressing, 36
   how caused, 37
Confiscation, 169
Connecticut, rent and taxes in, 150-152
Consumers, of sugar, taxed, 12
   of whisky, 12
Corruption, political, 16-18
   result of crooked taxation, 9, 13, 15-18
      by whisky trust, 16, 18
      by sugar trust, 16
   natural taxation best remedy for past, 213, 214
      best guaranty against future, 216-218
Credits, can wealth be increased by? 50-52
   taxation of, 50-56
      useless labor, 52, 53
      corporate, 53
      individual, 55
      how evaded, 53, 54, 56
Crooked taxation, 6-38
   defined, 9, 10
   general effects of, 6-8
   profits of, 7

Crooked taxation, heavy on poor, 8
    light on rich, 8
    on sugar and whisky, 11, 12
    promotes waste, 8, 13
    difficulty of regulating, 14, 15
    political corruption from, 16-18
    iniquitous methods of collecting, 18-22
        monstrous penalties of, 19, 22
        shocking indecencies of, 20
        insults to women by, 20
        extortions through, 21
        enforced by spies, fraud, and blackmail, 22
    widens social chasm, 22
    gives profits to speculators, 23
    legislative tricks in, 24
    protective duties, 24
    excise duties, 26
    dealers' profits on, 26
    total burden of, 27
    proportion of, to income of people, 35
    incidence of, 35, 36
    concentration of wealth through, 36, 37
Currency problem, caused by bad taxation, 60-62

Debts cannot increase wealth, 51
Deposits. See *Banks*
Direct taxation, 39
    practicable, 39
    always adopted by new communities, 39, 40
    on incomes, 41-45. See *Income tax*
    on successions, 45-48. See *Succession tax*
    on personal property, 49-105. See *Personal property*
    on improvements, 106-114. See *Improvements*
    on ground rents. See *Natural taxation*

Earnings of people of United States, 28-30

Economical government, impossible under crooked taxation, 13
    not promoted by taxing labor, 37
Effects of natural taxation, 199–223
    in general, 199, 221–223
    stimulus to production, 199, 200
    on wages, 201–204
        real, 201
        in money, 202, 203
        amount of rise, 203
    on capital, 204–206
    on security to property, 206–209
    on railway problem, 209
    on monopolies, 210
    on watered stocks, 211
    on corrupt grants, 212–214
    on usurped lands, 215
    on reform in government, 216–218
    on bribery, 217
    on tenement houses, 218–221
    generally, 221–223
Embargo of 1807, 14
England, taxation of personal property in, 70
Enough, one tax, 136–164
    adverse views considered, 136–139
    in Boston, 138, 152–156
    in Great Britain, 143–145
    in United States, 145–147
    in Pennsylvania, 147–150
    in Connecticut, 150–152
    generally, 156–158
    in rural districts, 158
Europe, taxation of personal property in, 70
Excisemen hated, 19
Excise taxes, methods of collecting, 19
    burdens resulting from, 26

Experience, testimony of, 70-83
    of England, 70
    of Rome, 73
    of Spain, 73
    of New York, 75
    of California, 76-81
    of Boston, 81-83
    of Ohio, 88-97
    of Missouri, 98

Farmers, hold most visible chattels, 63
    effect of personalty tax on, 84-100
    believe in personalty taxes, 84, 183
        taxing everything, 183
    personal property of, 85-87
    ideas of, 86
    errors of, 87
    Ohio, experience of, 88-98
    pay largest share of taxes, on personalty, 88-90, 96, 98
    Missouri, experience of, 98
        on credits, 90-92, 95
        on money, 93, 95, 97
        reasons why, 99, 100
    improvements, 108, 111
    American, defined, 182, 183
    their opinions, 183
    assumed to be all farm-owners, 183
    ceasing to own land, 184
    a declining political factor, 184, 185
    lose by taxing improvements, 185-191
    proportion of land values of, 187-190
    compared with city owners, 190
    gain under natural taxation, 191-193
    relieved, without injustice to others, 193
    Massachusetts, 194-198
        insist on paying heavy taxes, 196, 197

Farms, taxed more heavily than cities, 88–100, 196, 197
  assessment of, 188–190
  statistics of Massachusetts, 194–198
  value of improvements in, 187
Franchises, taxation of, 124–128
  railway, 125–127
  telegraph, 127
  gas, electric, etc., 127
  untaxed, 128
  bribe-bought, 210, 212–214

General property tax, 49
  See *Personal property*
Gibbon's *History of Rome*, 73
Giffen, Robert, 143
Government, ground rent, depends on, 116
              varies with cost of, 116
              should pay for, 119
              should pay only fair cost of, 132–134
              sufficient for cost of, 136–164
  cost of. See *Taxes*
  gives all land value, 158, 159
  necessary, cannot cost more than rent, 159–164
  proper distribution of cost of, 160–164
Great Britain and Ireland, rents and taxes in, 136, 137, 143–145
  land values in, 144
Greeley, Horace, 13
Ground rent, what it is, 116
  Ricardo on, 116, 117
  justice of, 117
  taxation of, 119
    equality of, 120
    practicable, 121
    accuracy in, 121
    effect on monopolies, 125–128
    cannot be shifted, 129–132

Ground rent, taxation of, amount of, 132
    sharing benefits of, 134
  amount of, in Great Britain and Ireland, 136, 137, 143, 144
    in Boston, 138, 152–156
    in United States, 143–147
    in Pennsylvania, 147–150
    in Connecticut, 150–152
    in rural districts, 158
    exceeds cost of government, 159, 162–164
    in new territories, 167, 168
  delegated taxation, 165
  ought to bear all taxes, 166
  no claim to exemption, 172
Gunton, George, on rent, 137

Harris, William T., on rent, 137
Hudson, Frederick, on railways, 210

Improvements, taxation of, 106
    a tax on chattels, 106
    not direct taxation, 106–109
      on buildings, 107
      falls on tenant, 108
      on cultivation, 108
        consumers, 109
    injurious to public, 109
    discourages production, 110
      beauty, 110, 111
      repairs, 110, 111
    punishes improvement, 110–112
    causes bad building, 111
    equality of, impracticable, 112–114
    effect on farmers, 185–198. See *Assessments; Farmers*
    none under natural taxation, 207

Incidence of taxation, under present system, 35
    by classes, 36
  under natural tax, 174
    on landless, 177
    on land-owners, 177–182
    on largest land-owners, 181
    on owners of vacant land, 182
    on farmers, 182–194. See *Farmers*
  See *Burden of taxation*
Income of United States, 28–35
  for 1866, 31
  for 1880, 32
Income tax, returns, in United States, 30–32
  in Great Britain, 33
  general, induces perjury, 41, 45
    always evaded, 41, 42
    excuses for, 42
    not all direct tax, 43, 44
    unfit for local use, 44
Indirect taxation, 6–38
  taxes on improvements, 107–109
  See *Crooked taxation*
Injustice, justice remedy for, 210, 216
Inventors entitled to wealth, 211

Justice of natural taxation, 165–173
  privilege implies duty, 165, 166
  illustrations, 166–168
  objections to, 169
    confiscation, 169
    class legislation, 169
    compensation, 170–173

Landless class in United States, 175, 176
  gain by taxation of ground rents, 177

Landlords, natural tax-gatherers, 118
    taxes on, 119, 129-134
    denouncing tax on rent, 129
    cannot recover rent-tax, 129-131
    can recover house-tax, 131
    benefits of rent-tax to, 134, 135
Land-owners in United States, 175, 176
    effect of taxation of ground rents on, 147, 177-182
    gain by most, 178
    different classes of, 180
    loss by a few, 180, 181
Land, usurped, 215
Land values, what, 71, 126, 127
    taxes on, 119-134, 136-164
    how ascertained, 139, 140
    proportion in real estate, 141-143
        See *Ground rent; Natural taxation.*
    in Great Britain, 136, 137, 143, 144
    in Boston, 138, 152-156
    in United States, 143-147
    in Pennsylvania, 147-150
    in Connecticut, 150-152
    in rural districts, 158
    in new territories, 167, 168

Mallock, W. H., 136, 139
Massachusetts, expenses of small towns in, 163
    farm values, 194-198
    city values, 195, 196
    farmers insist on paying largest share of taxes, 196, 197
McLeod, H. D., theory of credits, 50
Merchandise, assessment of, 65
    would vanish, 67
Mistakes in new tariffs, 23
    profits made out of, 23

INDEX.

Money, taxation of, 57–60
    in bank, 57
    paper, 58
    coin, 58
    scarcity of, 60, 61
    demand for more, 61
    problem result of bad taxation, 60–62
Monopolies, best cure for, 210–216
    See *Franchises ; Railways*

Natural taxation, 115–135
    what it is, 115
    automatic, 115
    irresistible, 115, 118
    ground rent is, 116
        defined, 116, 117
        Ricardo on, 116, 117 note
        justice of, 117, 118
        who receive, 118, 119
        should pay all expenses, 119
        assessment of, 121–124. See *Assessments*
    collection free from objectionable methods, 120
    on franchises and monopolies, 124–128
        See *Franchises*
    cannot be shifted, 129–132
    amount of, 132
    benefits of, shared with landlords, 134
    effects of, 199–223. See *Effects of natural taxation*

Oaths, taxation by, 74–77
    reverence for, 74, 102
Oklahoma, opening of, 167, 172
    original taxes in, 167
    ground rents in, 168
    landlords and taxes in, 168

Pennsylvania, rents and taxes in, 147-150
    land values in, 148, 150
Perry, Professor, 1
Personal property, taxation of, 49-105
    credits, 50-57. See *Credits*
    money, 57-60. See *Money*
    banks, 60-62. See *Banks*
    visible chattels, 62-69. See *Chattels*
    merchandise, 64-68. See *Merchandise*
    assessments for, 63-69 See *Assessments*
    history of, 70, 72, 73
    experience of, 70-100
    always a failure, 72-83
    Roman methods, 73
    Spanish methods, 73
    American methods, 73-83
    by oath, 74
    perjury under, 74, 76, 77
    in New York, 75
    in California, 76-81
    in Boston, 81, 82
    in Illinois, 83
    in Ohio, 88-98
    in Missouri, 98, 99
    effect on farmers, 84-100. See *Farmers*
    effect on women and children, 101-105. See *Women*
Philadelphia, land values in, 141, 142
Poverty, taxation of, 8
Problems, currency, 60
    tenement-house, 218-221
Production, stimulated by natural taxation, 199, 200
Professors on taxation, 1
Profits, on tariff taxes, 23-26
    on excise taxes, 26
    on indirect taxes, 26, 27
    amount of, 27

Profits, increased by tax reform, 205
Property, security of, under natural taxation, 206
Protective taxes, profits made out of, 24
    burdens resulting from, 24–26

Railways, franchises of, 125–127
    problem of, 209
    "watered" stocks, 211
    street, franchises, 212
    Broadway, 214
    remedy for corrupt grants of, 212–214
Reform, in government, 216
    "a mere fiscal," 210
Rich and poor, taxation on, 8, 22–37
Robbery, vested rights in, 6, 7
Roman taxation, 73

Savings of people of United States, 33–35
Shaw, Chief-Justice, 155
Social chasm, result of crooked taxation, 22–37
Stocks, "watered," 211
Succession tax, 45–48
    popularity of, 45
    how evaded, 46
    not fit for exclusive tax, 46
    oppressive on widows, 46, 47
    leads to public waste, 47
Sufficiency of natural taxation, 136–164
    See *Enough, One tax*
Sugar, taxes on, 11, 12
Sumner, Professor, 1

Taxation. See *Bad taxation ; Burden ; Crooked taxation ; Direct taxation ; Effects ; Enough, one tax ; Improvements ; Incidence ; Justice ; Natural taxation ; Personal property ; Women*

Taxes, in Boston, 138
    in Great Britain, 143
    in United States, 147
    in Pennsylvania, 148, 149
    in Connecticut, 150, 151
    in Boston, 152, 153
    proportion of, to ground rents, 136, 138, 145, 147, 149, 150, 152, 153, 156, 157

Tenants, willing to pay rent, 115
    competition of, 115
    do not pay too much, 117
    rent-tax not shifted on, 129–132
    house-tax shifted on, 131
    sub-letting, 132
    influences reducing rent of, 134

Tenement-house problem, 218–221

Trustees, taxation of, 102, 103
    pious scruples of, 102
    wicked, 103

United States, rents and taxes in, 145–147
    classes in, 174–176
    families in, 175
    land-owners in, 175, 176
    landless in, 175, 176
    tenants in, 175
    landless voters in, 176

Vanderbilt, Cornelius, 112

Wages, effect of natural taxation on, 201–204
    immigration and, 202
    of domestics, 203
    probable amount of rise in, 203

Wells, David A., 25, 74, 112

Western Union Telegraph Co., 127

Whisky tax, 11, 12
    corruption in, 18
Women, taxation of, 101–105
        heavier than on men, 75, 101, 104, 105
        through trustees, 102
    returns honest, 103
    stripped by tax-searchers, 20
    clothing exposed, 20
        taxed and seized, 21
    insults and oppressions of, 20, 21
    oppressed by succession tax, 46

www.ingramcontent.com/pod-product-compliance
Lightning Source LLC
Chambersburg PA
CBHW022007220426
43663CB00007B/991